English Life in the
Seventeenth Century

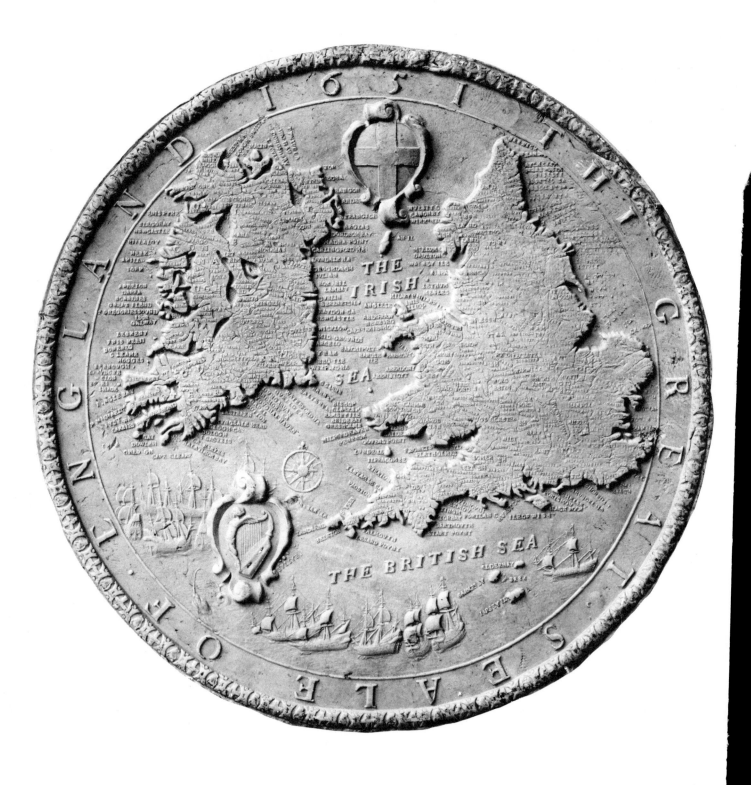

English Life
in the
Seventeenth Century

Roger Hart

"As one who long in populous city pent,
Where houses thick and sewers annoyt the air,
Forth issuing on a summer's morn to breathe
Among the pleasant villages and farms
Adjoin'd, from each thing met conceives delight."
(John Milton, *Paradise Lost*)

WAYLAND PUBLISHERS LONDON

THE ENGLISH LIFE SERIES

English Life in the Seventeenth Century
English Life in the Eighteenth Century
English Life in the Nineteenth Century

Roger Hart

SBN 85340 001 6

Copyright © 1970 by Roger Hart
First published 1970 by
Wayland (Publishers) Ltd
101 Grays Inn Road London WC1

Printed and bound in Great Britain by Jarrold and Sons Ltd.,
Norwich

Contents

PREFACE

When King James I came to the throne in 1603 his English subjects only numbered about four and a half millions. But by and large the country was a prosperous one. Merchants, gentry, tradespeople and small-holders thanked the stability of the long reign of Elizabeth I, a flourishing wool trade and English maritime supremacy for the material benefits of life. Yet seventeenth-century England faced a grave crisis of Church and government which overshadowed everyone's lives. The Elizabethan religious settlement had not healed the rifts between Catholics, Protestants and Puritans. The personal kingship of James I and Charles I, alienating Parliament and much of the people, at last led England into Civil War. It is not the purpose of this book to discuss the complex public debates of this period, nor its tangled political history, but rather to study the quality of life for ordinary people of different classes, and in different occupations, from the lifetime of Shakespeare in the early years of the century to the Restoration period and after. In these pages, illustrated with many contemporary pictures, we shall study English home life, the life of working people in the towns and in the countryside during the years of peace and Civil Wars, fashions and manners, religious and moral attitudes, sports and recreations, education, travel, and the disasters of plague and fire which overtook London after the Restoration. We are lucky to have the writings of a variety of contemporaries – Evelyn, Pepys, Clarendon, Defoe, Chamberlayne, Howell, Walton and many others – to illuminate the character of their times, and to show us how by the end of the seventeenth century England had not only advanced in material terms, but had found a greater degree of stability and tolerance in everyday life.

I Jacobean England

THE OPENING YEARS of the seventeenth century marked the end of a golden era. For on 24th March, 1603, between the hours of two and three in the morning, Queen Elizabeth I died, surrounded by her physicians, "as the most resplendent sun setteth at last in a western cloud." The Queen was dead, long live the King. Shortly before her death, "Gloriana" had performed her last act of state, by naming James VI of Scotland as her successor. The Tudor dynasty was over, the troubled times of the Stuarts were about to begin.

The people of England waited in uncertainty, to see whether the dead Queen's wishes would be respected. The accession of James of Scotland was, however, a peaceful one, and a contemporary wrote that "the like joy, both in London and all parts of England, was never known." James himself had intended that this should be so, and planned the first few months of his reign with some care. Whatever he secretly felt of his "upstart" Parliament, he began by treating them with great courtesy. "Chairs for the ambassadors," he called on one famous occasion, while receiving a Parliamentary deputation. The gentry were gratified to learn of his interest in hunting; most courtiers were relieved when he summoned Robert Cecil (1550–1612) to serve him as faithfully as he had Elizabeth.

James reinforced the popularity of his first few months by the wholesale distribution of honours. In eight weeks he created as many new knights as Queen Elizabeth had done in the previous ten years, and Sir Francis Bacon (1561–1629) wrote sadly to Robert Cecil, the Lord Treasurer, of "this almost prostituted title of knighthood;" peerages were sold, too, at £10,000 apiece.

Jacobean London

What sort of capital did James inherit in the spring of 1603? During Elizabeth's reign, towards the end of the previous century, efforts had been made to limit the sprawl of London's outskirts. A Royal Proclamation explained that the Queen had seen "the City of London and the suburbs and confines thereof to increase daily by access of people to inhabit the same." Small rooms housed sometimes dozens of poor people, who "must live of begging, or of worse means; and they heaped

Top Death of Elizabeth I at Richmond in 1603. *Above* James I medal commemorating peace with Spain, 1604

The Thames with London Bridge, from Visscher's *Map of London* (1620)

St. Dunston in the east

Allhallows Berking

Hackny

Stepny

The Tower

Lyon Key

Billingate

Bridge Gate

St Olaf

9

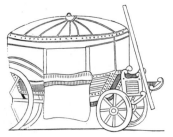

A seventeenth-century coach

A sedan chair

Sedan chair carrier

Above and below Coaches of around 1600

Below Sedan chair of Charles I's time

up together, and in a sort smothered with many families of children and servants in one small house or tenement."

It followed that "if any plague or popular sickness should by God's permission enter among those multitudes, the same should not only spread itself and invade the whole city and confines . . . but would also be dispersed through all other parts of the realm." Few people could have guessed just how terrible a toll was to be taken in 1665, the year of the Great Plague.

Every class of London citizen shared the same hazard of bubonic plague, a shadow which for generations had darkened metropolitan life. In the very first year of James I's reign, his coronation year, a London plague took a severe toll of life. Those of the nobility who had fashionable town houses along the Strand, by the River Thames, suffered like the poor; some sought sanctuary in the hamlets of Hampstead and Highgate, on hills near London, a few miles from St. Paul's Cathedral.

Beggars were numerous throughout seventeenth-century England

The population of seventeenth-century London was about half a million, mostly packed into rotten wood and plaster houses in narrow streets filled with decaying refuse. The first thing a twentieth-century visitor would have noticed would undoubtedly have been the stench. As late as 1661 John Evelyn complained that "this horrid smoke obscures our churches and makes our palaces look old. It fouls our clothes and corrupts the waters, so that the very rain and refreshing dews that fall in the several seasons precipitate this impure vapour, which with its black and tenacious quality, spots and contaminates whatever is exposed to it."

He added, "That this glorious and ancient city . . . should wrap her stately head in clouds of smoke and sulphur, so full of stink and darkness, I deplore with just indignation. That the buildings should be composed of such a congestion of mis-shapen and extravagant houses; that the streets should be so narrow and incommodious in the very centre, and busiest places of intercourse; that there should be so ill and uneasy a form of paving underfoot, so troublesome and malicious a disposure of the spouts and gutters overhead, are particularly worthy of reproof and reformation; because it is hereby rendered a labyrinth in its principal passages, and a continual wet day after the storm is over."

City records frequently refer to the appalling state of the sewage. The Fleet River, or Ditch as it was often called, was the worst of the small tributary streams that brought sewage to the River Thames. In the seventeenth century the Fleet was still an open river, and its obnoxious fumes were a reproach to public health. Alexander Pope was later to write in the *Dunciad* (1728):

> . . . Fleet Ditch, with disemboguing streams
> Rolls the large tribute of dead dogs to the Thames,
> The King of dykes! – than whom no sluice of mud
> With deeper sable blots the silver flood.

Lady carried in a chair

In Shakespeare's day London was a small city with open country

A London street in 1600

only a few minutes away. Crowded gabled houses overhung the maze of narrow cobbled streets and alleys, dominated by the great landmark of St. Paul's Cathedral, which also served as a popular meeting place. The three main shopping centres – Fleet Street, Cheapside, and Holborn – lay close at hand.

Many contemporaries noted the rise of coaches and carriages in the early 1600s. Thomas Middleton and Thomas Dekker wrote in *The Roaring Girl* (1611): "They keep a vile swaggering in coaches nowadays; the highways are stopped with them." The streets of London had always been narrow, and growing wheeled and pedestrian traffic involved the city in a perpetual state of crisis. In those days, London had no planning or highways authority; each householder was supposed to keep in good repair the section of street that passed his own house.

Many books and pamphlets debated the state of roads and travel. One, *A Discourse on Leather* (1629), declared that the twin cities of London and Westminster had about five thousand "coaches and carouches" between them. Privately owned coaches frequently collided with hackney coaches which plied for hire. In 1636 a tract suggesting

A covered coach

a code of conduct was published under the title *Coach and Sedan Pleasantly Disputing for Place and Precedence*. London was a great stage-coach terminus. As the services to Bristol, Bath, Norwich, York, and other provincial destinations were relatively expensive, the economically minded would arrange to travel more cheaply aboard a horse-drawn freight waggon. These wide-wheeled vehicles did not make very fast time.

As the hub of commercial life, and home of the Court, London drew many visitors. Among the crowds of resident small tradesmen, shopkeepers, servants and others, there mingled beggars, wandering friars, and several thousand foreigners. Foreigners were treated in a cavalier fashion by most Londoners, as was the handful of Jews who ignored the ancient laws designed to keep them out.

London markets in 1598, *left* Billingsgate, *right* Eastcheap

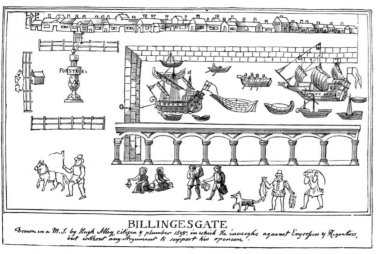

Countrywomen going to market

In the throng by St. Paul's street traders monotonously intoned their street cries and rang handbells to attract attention. Most bore their merchandise in barrows, trays, or sacks – fruit, vegetables, clothing, brooms, pins, vinegar, fresh water, and other household commodities. Many of the wooden houses opened their ground floors as shops, where goods could be displayed. The goods were often hand-made in a workshop to the rear – leather and metal goods, lengths of cloth, crude wooden furniture, pots and pans, and the like. Many of the traders bought their wares from hawkers who came into the city at dawn with heavy waggons from near-by villages and hamlets, bringing fresh fruit, vegetables, and dairy produce. Many of these hawkers sold their wares direct. Few Londoners kept their own animals, although one Westminster resident annoyed his neighbours by keeping cows in his kitchen. Traders tended to congregate in special areas – goldsmiths, for instance, in Cheapside, booksellers near St. Paul's.

A hat and basket seller in 1640

If a visitor from today could go to Jacobean London, he would not think much of the quality of the food on sale. Milk was rather thin, although asses' milk was sold at two or three shillings a pint. The ease of river travel explains why fish was usually fresh, and could be kept in open tanks for selection by the customer. There was no ice-packing in those days. Fish was a good deal cheaper than beef, which was beyond the purse of most Londoners as a regular item in the diet.

John Earle declared in his *Microcosmographie* (1628), that "Paul's Walk is the land's epitome." He explained, "It is the general mint, of all famous lies, which are here, like the legends of popery, first coined and stamped in the church. All inventions are emptied here, and not a few pockets." The playwright, Thomas Dekker, wrote in *Gull's Hornbook* (1609) that St. Paul's was the haunt of the fashionable young man. The best time to stroll there was "when the main shoal of islanders are swimming up and down." Dekker warned his readers to take care in the throng. If a young blood loitered by a pillar plastered with advertisements, he might easily be taken for someone wanting employment. Or, if he thoughtlessly stepped into the Cathedral wearing spurs, he would be made to pay the "spur money" traditionally claimed by the choir boys. He might pass his time by carving his name in the leaded roof, which already "contains more names than Stow's Chronicle" (John Stow's *Survey of London*).

London Inns and Taverns

London was famed for its inns and taverns, which played host to many classes of people – lawyers, merchants, writers, Parliamentarians, and other people in search of refreshment. In *Microcosmographie* (1628), John Earle preferred a tavern to a mere alehouse. "A tavern is a degree, or

London was renowned for its inns and taverns which in 1613 numbered more than a thousand

A meal in a tavern

if you will, a pair of stairs above an alehouse . . . it is the busy man's recreation, the melancholy man's sanctuary, the stranger's welcome, the Inns of Court man's entertainment, the scholar's kindness, and the citizen's courtesy."

In 1613 Sir Thomas Middleton counted more than a thousand London alehouses and taverns where a dinner might only cost three-pence. Other writers and visitors to London sometimes showed displeasure at the high prices in some establishments; but perhaps this simply echoed the great disparity of wealth within English society at that time. Yet, explained Henry Peacham in *The Worth of a Penny*, "the use of them is necessary, for if a man meets with his friend . . . whither should they go, having no friend's house near to go into, especially in rainy or foul weather, but to a tavern?" An official report of 1619 claimed that the population of Southwark was "chiefly of innkeepers."

The fare provided in taverns and alehouses was plain but substantial – beef, mutton, chicken, cabbage, pigeon pie, fish, ham, and various kinds of English pudding. Beverages included sack, wine, and ale. Inn yards bustled with activity, especially in the well-known coaching inns, where passengers jostled with coachmen, servants, maids, thieves, children, grooms, and passers-by.

Tobacco was a novelty of the period. Although Sir Francis Drake had imported tobacco in the reign of Queen Elizabeth I (to the amazement of his contemporaries), it did not really catch on until the seventeenth century. The London historian, James Howell, sent a pouch of tobacco to a friend, one New Year's day:

"To usher in again old Janus, I send you a parcel of Indian perfume, which the Spaniards call the Holy Herb, in regard of the various Virtues it hath; but we call it Tobacco; I will not say it grew under the King of Spain's window, but I am told it was gathered near his Gold-Mines of Potosi (where they report, that in some Places there is more of that Ore than Earth), therefore it must needs be precious Stuff.

"If moderately and seasonably taken (as I find you always do) 'tis good for many Things; it helps Digestion, taken a-while after Meat; a leaf or two being steeped o'er Night in a little White-wine is a Vomit

Beside food and drink many inns provided musicians and other entertainment for their guests

that never fails in its Operations; it is a good companion to one that converseth with dead Men; for if one hath been poring long upon a book, or is toil'd with the Pen, and stupify'd with study, it quickeneth him, and dispels those Clouds that usually o'erset the Brain."

A seventeenth-century tavern

He explains that its smoke was a wholesome scent which "o'er-masters all other smells, as King James, they say, found true, when being once a Hunting, a Shower of Rain drove him into a Pigsty for Shelter, where he caus'd a Pipeful to be taken on purpose; It cannot endure a Spider or a Flea, with such like Vermin, and if your Hawk be troubled with any such being blown into his feathers, it frees him; it is good to fortify and to preserve the sight, the smoke being let in round the Balls of the Eyes once a week, and frees them from all rheums, driving them back by way of Repercussion; being taken backward 'tis excellent good against the Cholic, and taken into the Stomach, it will heat and cleanse it."

The River Thames

In the seventeenth century, the River Thames was famous for its frost fairs. The waterworks at London Bridge had the effect of slowing the river's current above that point, and in a very cold winter the river would often freeze over. A contemporary wrote in *Great Frost* (1608) that the river was "an alley to walk upon without dread. . . . The citizen's wife that looks pale when she sits in a boat for fear of drowning, thinks that here she treads as safe now as in her parlour."

The frosts were a menace to those who depended on the Thames for their living – watermen, fishermen, Newcastle coal merchants, and merchants shipping cargoes of fresh foods. But they afforded entertainment to most people. Showmen erected penny booths on the ice, barbers shaved their customers, and innkeepers set up tavern-tents. The diarist, John Evelyn, noted the shops "full of commodities." The greatest frost was that of 1698, when the ice lay so thick that a coach-and-six rolled across from one bank to the other.

Lambeth Palace in London, 1647

The River Thames gave a living to thousands of fishermen. A few of these were wealthy entrepreneurs owning dozens of boats and a household full of clerks and apprentices. But most fished from a single boat, which in some cases provided their only permanent home. Thames fishermen sold each day's catch to Billingsgate traders, who then wholesaled it to the City fishmongers for hawking on a commission basis in the streets or in small shops. Donald Lupton wrote in 1632 that the Thames "is the privileged place for fish and ships, the glory and wealth of the city, the highway to the sea, the bringer-in of wealth and strangers . . . he is a little sea and a great river."

John Taylor declared in *An Arrant Thief* (1632) that the Thames watermen (ferrymen) were suffering from growing competition from wheeled transport through the streets of the metropolis:

All sorts of men work all the means they can
To make a "Thief" of every waterman,
And as it were in one consent they join
To trot by land i' th' dirt and save their coin.
. . . Against the ground, we stand and knock our heels,
Whilst all our profit runs away on wheels.

Although watermen had ferried customers over and along the Thames for many generations, not until the sixteenth century had they become a thriving community, proud of their own chartered Company with its hall in the City of London. John Taylor himself had fallen victim to the risk facing all watermen – that of being "pressed" against their will into naval service. Some master-watermen deliberately arranged for their apprentices to be pressed, since the unlucky youths then had to turn

Ciuitatis Westmonasteriensis pars.

Parlament House   the Hall   the Abby

Westminster from the Thames, 1647

over any prize money gained at sea. John Taylor spent much of his time defending his fellow-watermen. "A waterman cannot be false to his trade," he cleverly explained, "for he has no weights or measures to falsify, nor can he curtail a man's passage."

Until destroyed in the Great Fire of 1666, the old London Bridge was one of the sights of London, indeed of Europe. Fynes Moryson declared in his *Itinerary* (1617), that "the bridge at London is worthily to be numbered among the miracles of the world." The bridge carried a great superstructure of houses and shops, several storeys high. Between one and two hundred persons lived and worked there. The bulwarks and arches with their watermills, however, constituted a menace to small river vessels, which were sometimes damaged while navigating their way through the narrow arches and fast-running currents.

17

Strolling players entertain passers-by on the Thames' banks at Richmond

Traitors' heads, traditionally exhibited on spikes, sometimes gave the bridge a horrific aspect.

Shakespeare's Theatre

The writer Thomas Coriat (1577–1617) held a high opinion of the London theatre in 1611. Nothing, he said, could compare "for apparel shows of music" of "our stately playhouses in England." The stage offered a very cheap form of entertainment: standing admission cost one penny, although a seat cost extra. Additional payments were necessary for cushions to sit on, or to reserve a stall at the side of the stage. Shortly before the play began, trumpets played a fan-fare so that everyone could take his seat. When everyone was settled, attendants walked up and down and collected the admission money which was then put into locked boxes (hence "box office"). Plays were generally held in the afternoon while daylight remained. If the plays continued into dusk, light was sometimes provided by burning pitch or tar. Several wooden playhouses were accidentally burned to the ground, as a result.

Great actors were accustomed to fame and renown. When the actor Richard Burbage died in 1619 he was said to be worth £300 a year, a small fortune for those days. Edward Alleyn, another, did well enough to buy a £10,000 estate at Dulwich, where he founded a college. The wardrobes of some actors compared with those of their noble patrons.

Shakespeare was one of the playwright actors skilled at giving old plays a topical interest. The biographer Donald Lupton wrote in 1632, "They are as crafty with an old play as bawds with old faces. The one puts on a new fresh colour, and the other a new face and name."

Audiences were loud and noisy. Thomas Dekker pointed out in 1609, "Your carman and tinker claim a stronger voice, in their suffrage to sit, to give judgement on the play's life and death as well as the proudest Momus among the tribe of critic." During the performance, people walked about the playhouse or stood by the pillars eating and drinking, or filling the auditorium with thick blue tobacco smoke. (The Puritans took special exception to these habits.)

Opposite: top Seventeenth-century London's bridge was as crowded with houses as the city's streets; *left* fresh fish from London's river; *right, above* the customs house in London, 1598; *right, below* the Tower

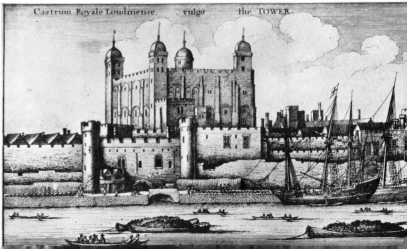

Castrum Royale Londinense, vulgo the TOWER.

In the early years of the seventeenth century the stage enjoyed a great popularity, and not until 1642 did Puritan pressure succeed in closing playhouses down. The theatre, like the other arts, flourished in a climate of aristocratic patronage. Indeed, specially commissioned masques and revels enlivened many great private receptions in London. These masques preferred an elegance and sophistication which was lacking on the popular stage, and the promoters took far more care with the music and stage settings. The greatest masque impresarios were, perhaps, Ben Jonson (1574–1637) and Inigo Jones (1572–1652), whose *Masque of Blackness* was performed for the royal court at Whitehall on twelfth night in 1605.

London's Swan playhouse in 1596

Male Dress

"When your posterity shall see our pictures they shall think we were foolishly proud of apparel." So thought one Richard Rowlands in the year 1605. When Rowlands made this remark the usual dress for men was the doublet and hose. For those who could afford it, the doublet was a close-fitting, long-waisted waistcoat, the front of which was padded out with a thick material like buckram or canvas. In Shakespeare's time (died 1616) the doublet was often slashed and quilted, although during the reign of Charles I (1625–49) the old heavy paddings gave way to a simpler, more severe, style. The skirt of the doublet was usually flared out over the breeches, the doublet itself tight at the neck. "The collar of it (his doublet) rose up so high and sharp as if it would have cut his throat by daylight." (Thomas Middleton, 1604.) The doublet was fastened by a close row of hand-worked buttons down from the collar to the waist, and held with a low belt. Poor people would fasten their doublets with pins instead of buttons.

Here is a tailor's bill for a suit of Shakespeare's time: "Paid for seven yards of ash collar satin to make him a doublet and hose at fourteen shillings the yard. . . . Paid for three yards quarter of cloth to make him a cloak at eleven shillings the yard. Paid for a pair of silk stockings for him twenty-five shillings. Paid for taffeta to face and line the skirts of his doublet five shillings and fourpence. Paid for three dozen of buttons for it and his cloak." Until the end of the reign of James II (1688) the doublet and hose were usually worn with a sword belt with elaborate hangers.

Morris dancer and musician, 1600

During cold winters, many men wore a waistcoat underneath the doublet for extra warmth; a satin waistcoat for the purpose might cost about thirty shillings. Out of doors men sometimes wore surcoats known as mandilions, cassocks, riding-coats, or gaberdines. These were all loose garments with wide sleeves. It was felt more elegant to wear a French, Dutch, or Spanish cloak, at least until about 1660. State officials and lawyers tended to wear long black gowns instead of cloaks. The ruff, which one traditionally associates with Elizabethan England, passed out of fashion about 1620, although lawyers continued to wear them for some time.

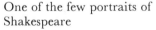

One of the few portraits of Shakespeare

The normal form of leg-wear for men in the first half of the century was either hose (footless stockings) or breeches. Hose eventually gave way to the stockings which became fashionable after the Restoration.

Opposite: top A London panorama, 1678; *centre* Greenwich Palace, 1620; *below* frost fair on the Thames 1683–84

London had many playhouses, the most famous were *left*, the Bear Garden and *right*, the Globe

Above and below Designs by Inigo Jones for a masque

Breeches were made in various styles, including Venetian, Calligaskin, Slop, Cloakbag, Spanish, and Open. Breeches were usually connected to the doublet by hooks and eyes, concealed under the waist of the doublet. Footwear included shoes, pumps, slippers, startups (high shoes), boots and buskins (knee boots), mostly made from oxhide. Rosettes were often worn on the toe of the shoe.

Head-gear was extremely varied, as pictures of the time show. It included the large cocked hat, the copotain (a hat with a high conical crown), and the sugar-loaf hat (worn with an uncocked brim). Hats were usually lined with velvet or taffeta, and trimmed with bands or cords of ribbon, silk, or cypress. The cap, which had been popular in Elizabethan England, went out of fashion by about 1610, although London apprentices and others continued to wear flat caps till about 1630.

In the first half of the century men wore their hair very long, usually down to the shoulders. "Your gallant is no man unless his hair be of the woman's fashion, dangling and waving over his shoulders." (Richard Rowlands, 1628.) The gallant often wore a love-lock on the forehead. Few people wore beards, although from about 1645 some began to cultivate moustaches. Those who did wear beards preferred the Vandyke style, pointed, and with waxed moustaches. Wigs belonged to the second half of the century.

Women's Fashions

Until about 1625 most women wore a dress consisting of a bodice and skirt, sometimes called a kirtle. Gowns were often worn over the bodice and skirt. After about 1625 the gown became a very important part of women's dress. Bodices were often worn low necked and were fastened down the front by buttons, ribbon bows, lacing, or a V-shaped gap closed by a "stomacher." The old Elizabethan square-necked bodice was rejected from about 1615. Plunging necklines caused much comment, then as now: "Your displayed breasts, with what shameless art they wooed the shamefast passenger." (*The English Gentlemen and The English Gentlewomen*, 1641.) High-necked bodices were also worn, and

Costumes of London citizens in 1640, fashions for the nobility and *second from left* the mayor and aldermen of the city council

like the low-necked versions were usually surmounted by a laced ruff. Bodices were worn very tight at the waist, and contrasted with long flowing sleeves which, like men's doublet sleeves, were often slashed and puffed around the arm. Women often wore jackets or waistcoats instead of bodices, especially for riding. These waistcoats were always heavily embroidered and fastened down the front in the same way as bodices.

Women from the upper ranks of society usually wore abundant petticoats or farthingales under their skirts which were rather like the Victorian crinoline. The farthingale was made of wire or whale-bone and often in the shape of a wheel around the waist. This gave early seventeenth-century dresses a rather tub-shaped appearance, the skirt falling more or less straight down to the ankles. Women, like men, wore ruffs at the neck until the 1620s. Women also wore hand-ruffs until about 1630, wide cuffs or frills at the wrist, cloaks, tippets (fur capes) or mantles, and a variety of hoods, hats, and lace handkerchiefs above the head. In Jacobean times women liked to wear their hair piled up high tied into a bun at the back, worn in a fringe at the forehead, and crimped and brushed on top.

Many kinds of make-up could be bought, paint, powder, and perfumes: "For a penny a chambermaid may buy as much red ochre as will serve seven years painting of her cheeks" (1641). Patches, too, which had come into fashion in about 1595, were growing in popularity. These were cut into amazing shapes and glued to the face: "Your black patches you wear variously, some cut like stars, some in half-moons, some in lozenges." (Beaumont and Fletcher, 1637.)

Women and men wore much the same kind of leg and footwear. Stockings were usually of knitted wool, and the most popular colour was apparently green. Socks and garters were also worn.

Fun was always made of country fashions *top and above right* by city dandies *top left and below*

The Jacobean Home

The seventeenth century saw a good deal of new building, and much money was spent on improving and modernizing old properties as well as building new ones. Stuart England had no planning restrictions, no land shortage, and no lack of good workmen. This was to become an

Fashions for London ladies, *left to right* at the end of Elizabeth I's reign,
a citizen's wife in 1649, a young girl and a gentlewoman in 1643

Above and below More exotic
fashions of the period

age of great architects, such as Inigo Jones, Sir Christopher Wren (1632–1723), and Sir John Vanbrugh (1672–1726). In the later years these men built great mansions as homes for the nobility and for the upper merchant classes. The "hall house" was a traditional type of design, common since Elizabethan times, and consisting of a central hall or chamber around which the smaller rooms and offices were placed. The hall was the heart of family life, dinners, entertainment, and servants' activities.

During the seventeenth century people began to demand smaller and warmer rooms, each designed for a particular purpose rather as in modern houses. In large manorial homes, the family preferred to eat in privacy, away from the demands of dependants, servants, and others for whom the house was the pivot of local life.

Furnishings in the Jacobean period tended to be plain and simple; for example, tables were of the bench or trestle type, curtains were seldom seen except as draught-covers on doors. Chairs were uncommon, too. As a rule, seating was afforded by long benches or wooden stools sometimes covered with leather, cloth, or quilts. In great households, however, splendid chairs were sometimes seen; for example, the rich armchair of Elizabethan times, the box chair, or elegant wickerwork chairs, or chairs with rush or cane seats. From the reign of James I, those who could afford it had their chairs upholstered with horse-hair padding or sometimes wool. Often skilfully embroidered in a tapestry design, upholstered chairs introduced new comfort to their Jacobean owners.

Householders often gave names to the different rooms, in rather the same way as taverns and inns. Family records sometimes refer to the Great Parlour, the Little Parlour, Winter Parlour, Oak Parlour, Matted Chamber, Blue Chamber, White Chamber, or Green Chamber. The floors were of plain polished wood without carpets (carpets for the entire floor were not introduced until the eighteenth century). The walls of the large rooms were often decorated with carved panels, or hung with rich tapestries. The greatest piece of furniture in an affluent home was the four-poster bed, hung with thick curtains and boasting an elaborately carved head-board and head-posts.

24

Second from left Mourning dress of an Elizabethan lady, and fashions for cooler weather in Stuart times

Great mansions often contained libraries, drawing-rooms, small private rooms, sometimes a salon. The long gallery of Elizabethan times remained popular, too. Lighted by a long row of windows, the long gallery was the display room for the art treasures of the house and musical instruments, and was used for dancing and other entertainments. The accommodation for servants was usually rather primitive, and the household staff usually slept upon rough pallets.

Bathrooms were rare in seventeenth-century England. They only began to appear towards the end of the century, usually in the houses of the great. The writer and traveller Celia Fiennes saw a great "bathe-ing room" at Chatsworth, the home of the Earls of Derby. Built with blue and white marble walls, the bath had "two locks to let in one hot, the other cold water, to attemper it as persons please." Soap was perfumed, and the water sweetened with herbs. In the first part of the century little thought was given to bathing, despite the pleas of a few like Sir John Harington, who wrote in *The Englishman's Doctor* (1608), "Love you to be cleane and well apparelled, for from which our cradles let us abhor uncleanness, which neither nature nor reason can endure." Toothbrushes were little used until well after the Restoration in 1660. Most people simply polished their teeth with cloths, and used ivory or wooden toothpicks. Despite the lack of dental care in those days, most people apparently kept their teeth well into old age – although a severe toothache could sometimes prove fatal through infection.

Gardens had first become a feature of English domestic life in Tudor times, and remained so throughout the seventeenth century. House-wives were proud of their herb gardens; tobacco was sometimes grown, although Francis Bacon had written that "English Tobacco hath small credit, as being too dull and earthy." Herbs were essential for both medicine and cooking. The kitchen garden was another necessity for good living. Vegetables such as carrots, beans, cabbages, peas, parsnips, onions, and pumpkins were developed, although mainly as soup ingredients rather than as dishes in themselves.

Large country mansions were often surrounded by vast private park-lands, which ensured some privacy, and a place where deer might be kept. But not until the eighteenth century, the age of Launcelot

The Elizabethan home, *left* Harvard House, Warwickshire, *right* Buckland Abbey, home of Drake

"Capability" Brown (1715–83), the landscape architect, did landscape gardening become fashionable.

The lady of a country house led a hard and varied life. The country house had to be an entirely self-supporting unit. Woodmen had to provide fuel; seamstresses had to make all the linen to supply the needs of the household; medicines had to be made up from herbs; and vegetables pickled.

The onset of winter was the signal for the careful laying up of bulk stores, so that the household could live until the spring, when the bad roads might become passable again, and contact with market towns renewed. The seventeenth-century housewife had no labour-saving devices as we know them. Every item had to be made and prepared by hand. The careful housewife made her kitchen staff set aside all waste animal fats, for use as tallow candles, and as a soap ingredient. Poultry feathers were cured for use in pillows and mattresses. A great

A contemporary print of masons at work

event in the household calendar was the "great wash" held every two to three months, when all the dirty linen would be brought to a stream or to large tubs, to be beaten by the laundrymaids.

The lady of the house had to study the arts of good management. She might have dozens of servants at her command – milkmaids, laundrymaids, cooks, seamstresses, messengers, footmen, grooms, and others. Her success rested upon familiarizing herself with every detail of the day's work.

Advice on running a household was traditionally handed down by mother to daughter – for example, prescriptions for herbal medicines, secret recipes for perfumes and aromatic waters, or the way to keep the household accounts. A lady might buy one of the many household books published in this period, such as Gervase Markham's *The English Huswife*. Markham made severe demands on his lady readers. They must be "of chaste thought, stout courage, patient, untired, watchful, diligent, witty, pleasant, constant in friendship, full of good neighbourhood, wise in discourse . . . secret in her affairs, comfortable in her counsels, and generally skilful in all the worthy knowledges which do belong to her vocation."

In the country, breakfast was generally taken between six and seven o'clock in the morning. It was a plain meal of meat, bread, and ale. Townspeople who could afford it might sometimes give breakfast parties, as Samuel Pepys did on New Year's Day, 1661, when he entertained his friends with a repast of oysters, neats' tongues (ox tongues), anchovies, wine, and Northdown ale.

The main meal of the day was dinner, served about noon. A great joint of beef, mutton, pork, or venison was placed on the table, or sometimes game – quail, pheasant, snipe, pigeon, or larks. The main course was eaten with an accompaniment of soups, salads, sauces, and then a variety of sweets – custards, jellies, and puddings.

If Thomas Fuller is to be believed, the poorer classes in the countryside ate as well, even if their diet was a plainer one. He wrote in 1642 that the farmer or yeoman "shall have as many joints as dishes; no

Left Picking hops for ale. *Right* a fanciful sketch of the Englishman's home

straggling joint of a sheep in the midst of a pasture of grasse, beset with sallads on every side, but solid, substantial food." Many famous local dishes were eaten – Yorkshire pudding, Lancashire hot pot, and the black puddings of the West Country.

Great houses took their meals amid a good deal of ceremony. Men wore their hats at the dinner table; the table was surrounded by servants of different ranks. Only knives were used to eat food, and in the absence of forks until late in the century, diners fed themselves with their hands; large communal finger bowls were provided by the waiters at the start and finish of the meal. The true Englishmen despised the Italian fork. Nicholas Breton wrote scornfully in *The Courtier and the Countryman*: "As for us in this country, when we have washed our hands after no foul work, nor handling any unwholesome thing, we need no little forks to make hay with our mouths, to throw our meat into them."

Left A family meal and *right* a supper party, hands and knives were the usual means of eating and forks, regarded as "nasty and foreign" were not common until the end of the century

Generally speaking, supper was a lighter and less elaborate affair, generally eaten between five and eight o'clock, and was a simpler version of the massive midday repast.

Marriage

Marriage among the gentry and the upper classes was planned more for its property settlements and family connexions than for any romantic reasons. Most parents made careful plans for the future of their children, and often made the arrangements while their children were still young. Sir Ralph Verney described "a young wedding between Lady Grace Grenville and Sir George Cartwright's grandson, which was consummated on Tuesday by the Bishop of Durham. She is six years old, and he a little above eight years old." Verney added that, in these circumstances, the newly weds would "carry themselves very gravely, and love dearly."

Certain days of the year were held to be lucky for weddings. They were as follows:

January	2, 4, 11, 19, 21	July	1, 3, 12, 19, 21, 31
February	1, 3, 10, 19, 21	August	2, 11, 18, 20, 30
March	3, 5, 12, 20, 23	September	1, 9, 11, 18, 28
April	2, 4, 12, 20, 22	October	1, 8, 15, 17, 27, 29
May	2, 4, 12, 20, 23	November	5, 11, 13, 22, 25
June	1, 3, 11, 19, 21	December	1, 8, 10, 19, 23, 29

When a daughter was betrothed by her father, the marriage settlement, or dowry, was agreed at the same time. A father was expected to settle on his daughter money or property appropriate to her station. In practice, the wife's property often came under the control of her new husband, although the settlement was intended as a guarantee of the daughter's future. Problems could often arise where a young man wished to marry "below his station": a small dowry with the bride would be an insult.

Left Vines were much more widely grown in England then than now.
Right A hostess in 1631 entertaining the guests from her bed

Most children followed their parents' wishes in marriage. Those few who broke away to marry someone of their own choice might have to face considerable parental wrath. Lord Cork angrily told his son that his wretched "selfishness" would "dash all my designs which concern myself and my house." On the other hand, if real antipathy existed between the young couple, few parents would insist on going through with the plans, on condition that a suitable alternative could be agreed.

In those days, families were often very large, and many daughters knew their parents could never afford a large dowry for them. Their lot was an unhappy one; many girls feared they would never be able to marry, let alone marry someone they liked. The most fortunate figure was the rich independent bachelor, who could afford to bide his time, and pick the best match he was offered.

Nor were these problems ended by the marriage day. Since most couples were married for reasons of family politics and advancement, with little romance, there was ample room for fraud and cruelty concerning the marriage settlement. Records of the day refer many times to husbands appropriating their wives' dowries for themselves; to wives

Hairstyle *above* and breeches *below*, of a fashionable man of the time

Above James I giving a banquet for the Spanish envoys during the negotiations for the marriage of his son to the sister of the king of Spain, 1622

Below The ceremonial entry of Prince Charles into Madrid in 1623

Fashionable shoes of the period, *above* for a woman, *below* for a man

A girl's dowry was often kept in chests like the Nonesuch chest

claiming large sums from their husbands when only a small dowry had been settled on them. Often enough, the parents must have felt that the marriage had not fulfilled its purpose.

In the seventeenth century the law stated that girls had to be at least twelve years old and boys fourteen on the day of the wedding. However, as we have seen, children could be betrothed to one another at much earlier ages than this, often when they were still in the nursery. When children were married in their early teens they often returned home for two or three years to their parents until they were considered old enough to start their married life.

Yet, despite all these conventions, marriage seems to have been a stable institution. Of course married couples separated then, as now, but a wife or husband who left his partner would be strongly criticized by contemporaries. A legal separation could be obtained from the courts of law, but such cases were uncommon. Marriage was intended to be for life and the sacred vows sworn during the marriage ceremony were taken very seriously. Divorce could only be obtained by a private act of Parliament, involving much difficulty and expense. There were no divorce courts as we know them.

Except in the case of Puritan marriages, weddings were staged as lavishly as the families could afford. Poor families sometimes held a "bride ale" to help overcome the expense; home brewed ale was sold to the wedding guests, many of whom brought gifts of food and drink for the party. Provincial areas had their own marriage customs. In Cheshire, for example, wedding guests traditionally visited the bride's home on the eve of the wedding and placed branches of trees or bushes on the doors and chimneys, to bring good luck.

The ceremony in church was much the same then as it is today. But in those days the custom was to throw flowers and sweet herbs in the path of the bride and, in the case of the groom, symbols of his trade. For example, wood shavings were spread in front of a carpenter, or grass in front of a farmer. Paper confetti was unknown, but instead the guests often threw handfuls of wheat over the heads of the married couple. At the end of all the celebrations, the couple were escorted to the bridal chamber with much cheerful encouragement, and the guests then withdrew to continue carousing downstairs.

A bed of Charles II's time, Hampton Court Palace

St. Valentine's day was celebrated each year on 14th February and became very popular with unmarried and married alike. Some husbands had their own wives as Valentines; Samuel Pepys did for two years running, giving his wife £5 the first time, and the second a Turkey stone set with diamonds. In 1629 James Howell wrote these lines to his Valentine:

> As 'mongst all Flow'rs the Rose excels,
> As amber 'mongst the fragrant'st smells,
> As 'mongst all Minerals the Gold,
> As marble 'mongst the finest Mould,
> As Diamonds 'mongst jewels bright,
> As Cynthia 'mongst the lesser Lights;
> > So 'mongst the Northern Beauties shine,
> > So far excels my Valentine.
>
> Here may be seen pure white and red,
> Not by feign's Art, but Nature wed,
> No simp'ring Smiles, no mimic Face,
> Affecture Gesture, or forc'd Grace,
> A fair smooth front, free from least Wrinkle,
> Her eyes (on me) like Stars do twinkle;
> > Thus all perfections do combine
> > To beautify my Valentine.

The aristocracy took much interest and pride in their family trees, often having them elaborately illustrated and bound

Opposite James I had been King of Scotland before ascending the English throne on the death of Elizabeth I in 1603. A portrait by the Flemish artist Daniel Mytens painted in 1621

32

The palace of Nonesuch in Surrey. Built by Henry VIII it was never completed, and today nothing remains of its much vaunted beauties except a few plans and paintings

Above Scenes of early seventeenth-century English country life from the Bedford table carpet, a type of table covering popular until about 1625. Both wind and watermills were used to grind grain for flour and guns appear popular for game shooting. *Opposite* The Soest portrait of William Shakespeare

London's winter highlights included the great frost fairs held on the frozen River Thames. This one, painted by Abraham Hondius, took place at the Temple stairs in 1684. On the far left is St. Clement's Danes Church and the Temple Church is on the far right

2 Freedom and Conscience

THE SEVENTEENTH CENTURY was a time of great religious troubles. A century before, Henry VIII (1509–47) had reformed the English Church and asserted his own Protestant supremacy and equality with Rome. In the reigns of his two children, first the sickly Protestant Edward VI (1547–53), and then the determined Catholic Mary (1553–58), England was plunged into years of bloody persecution and fanaticism. Moderate Protestants, zealous Puritan reformers and Catholics bitterly fought for control of national religious policies. The long reign of Elizabeth I (1558–1603), however, had restored some stability and created a new climate of moderate Protestantism, based upon the idea of uniformity. Individual churchgoers could, within reason, follow their spiritual preferences inside the framework of the Church of England.

It was the tragedy of the early seventeenth century that much of this good work was undone. Although coming from a Presbyterian kingdom (Scotland), James had no time for Puritanism and dreamed of restoring an authoritarian monarchy and church. His insistence on the divine rights of kings, and apostolic succession of bishops, alienated a largely Puritan Parliament – a Parliament on which he largely depended for his financial and foreign policies. Who were these Puritans that James so disliked?

Puritans

Deeply committed Puritans rejected not only the "popery" of the Catholics and their foreign allegiance to the Bishop of Rome, but also moderate Protestant attitudes. True, Puritans shared with other Protestants a common dislike of Catholicism, and a belief in the independence of the English Church from European influences; and they shared a growing hostility toward the unrepentant authoritarianism of James I and Charles I.

But Puritan beliefs went further. The Protestant Reformation must be carried on, and the Church of England further purified (hence "Puritan"). In Puritan eyes, every outward religious show was an idolatry and a blasphemy. Every church building, from the great cathedrals down to the parish churches were "mere steeple houses." One of the practical virtues of Protestantism was that it tolerated a fairly

Opposite Henrietta Maria, the French Catholic Princess whom Charles I married in 1625

wide range of religious observance, from extremes which today would be called high and low church. But most Puritans refused to compromise. They bitterly condemned the altars found in most English parishes, decked with white altar cloths, candles, and other sinful decorations; they condemned many of the old forms of prayer in the Prayer Book; they condemned the bishops' claims to an apostolic succession from St. Peter and attacked the whole structure of traditional church government. The Presbyterians wanted to do away with the bishops altogether.

In 1603 a body of Puritan priests presented the Millenary Petition to Parliament (so called, because a thousand priests were said to have subscribed to it). The Petition urged the Church to give up certain

Left A Puritan family; *right* a Puritan satire on the status of men of God and more worldly people

"impure" practices, such as making the sign of the cross at baptism, or placing the ring on the finger at weddings; priests were urged not to wear the cap and surplice. In fact, many Puritan priests had already dispensed with these customs in their own parishes up and down the country, and now sought official support for their action. The following year, King James I himself presided over a conference at Hampton Court, where the arguments of the bishops and the Puritan priests were hotly debated. James himself had no stomach for the Puritan outlook, and coined the phrase, "No bishop, no king," meaning that the episcopacy and the monarchy were indissoluble.

Although the Hampton Court Conference gave rise to a famous translation of the Bible (the "Authorized" or "King James" version) it also had the effect of sharpening religious attitudes. The English bishops refused to simplify the Prayer Book in the ways sought by the Puritans. Instead they adopted a new policy of "conformity," whereby every priest in every parish was bound to acknowledge the Thirty-Nine Articles of the Church. Many Puritan ministers refused to do so, opposing for example the rule that communicants should kneel; some Puritans were removed from office. Conformity was not, however, a great success, and in 1637 Archbishop William Laud complained that parishioners entered church with no more reverence "than a tinker and his bitch come into an alehouse."

Unruly Puritan priests were banned from journalism and authorship, as well as from their pulpits. Expulsion from the pulpit was in many ways an effective remedy, for Puritans depended heavily upon preaching for spreading their ideas. In 1622 the Church instructed parish priests not to deviate from their texts into general controversy. Puritans who continued to defy authority, like William Prynne (1600–99), John Lilburne (1618–57), John Bastwick (1593–1648) and Henry Burton (1579–1648), were condemned to public mutilation, although most held to their faith even *in extremis*. Fastened in the pillory, Burton

John Bastwick a prominent Puritan

The Orthodox true Minister,   the Seducer and false Prophet.

The Puritans tried to enforce a strict observance of Sundays, ideally with taverns closed and long church services

pointed to the holes in the posts and cried, "Through these holes God can bring light to his church!" A woman bystander cried back, "There are many hundreds which by God's assistance would willingly suffer for the cause you suffer for this day!" So it was to prove.

Puritans fought hard for strict observance of the Lord's Day in every town and hamlet. One Puritan, Nicholas Bownd, said, "We are bound straitly to rest from all the ordinarie workes of our calling." May games, morris dances and other Sunday festivities were severely attacked from Puritan pulpits. In 1617 James himself intervened, and declared that every churchgoer had the right to indulge in lawful sports when the church service was over, and these were listed for everyone's guidance in *The Book of Sports*; it met a good deal of opposition in Yorkshire, Lancashire, and other growing Puritan strongholds.

In the first years of the reign of James I a group of Puritan separatists held regular religious meetings at Scrooby Manor in Nottinghamshire. As a result of private difficulties, a breakaway group emigrated to Amsterdam in 1608, and a further group to Leyden in 1609. The stricter religious climate of the Netherlands would, they hoped, accord more closely with their beliefs. However, both the Dutch and the

Henry Burton another Puritan leader

The Old Manor House at Scrooby in Nottinghamshire where many of the
Pilgrim Fathers' meetings were held

English groups became disillusioned. In 1620 they decided to voyage across the Atlantic to settle in the New World, as the colonists of Virginia had done before them. Like many others who sponsored long voyages, they formed a voluntary joint-stock company, in whose name all the practical arrangements were made.

In September, 1620, their ship, the 180-ton *Mayflower*, set sail from Plymouth. (Another ship, the smaller *Speedwell*, had been sabotaged.) The *Mayflower* carried thirty-five of the Leyden Puritans, and sixty-six from London and Southampton. The emigrants, led by William Bradford, William Brewster, and John Carver, shared various reasons for joining the voyage, some religious, some material. This early ballad expressed their hopes:

> To glorifie the Lord 'tis done,
>   And to no other end;
> He that would crosse so good a worke,
>   To God can be no friend.

And another called *The Zealous Puritan* (1639) declared of New Plymouth:

> There you may teach our hymns,
> Without the laws controulment:
> We need not fear the bishops there,
> Nor spiritual-courst inroulment;
> Nay, the surplice shall not fright us,
> Nor superstitious blindness.

Many other pilgrims followed in their wake, and within seventeen years the Plymouth Colony numbered 549. Many died, however, either on the voyage or on arrival, due to scurvy or malaria. Those who survived became the foundation and nucleus of a small and vigorous colony, governed by simple rules and a high code of conduct. New Plymouth Colony remained independent until absorbed into Massachusetts in 1691.

At home in England, the years between the Millenary Petition (1603) and 1640 marked a growing divergence between Puritan opinion and that of the conformists, a divergence exacerbated by the continued use

Opposite: top The Pilgrim Fathers leaving Delfshaven, Holland, for Plymouth in England and then the New World; *below* the busy port of Amsterdam was exchanged for the fastnesses of Cape Cod

of sanctions by the Church in diocesan and other courts, such as excommunication.

Parliament showed its strong Puritan elements, for example in its recurring demands for a war against Spain, as in 1620. A ballad entitled *Gallants to Bohemia* proclaimed:

And hye again to Neptune's seas
Where we'll have riches when we please!

Apart from the commercial prizes to be won in such a war, many Puritans saw in it a crusade against a major Catholic state. They disliked James's familiarity with the Spanish ambassador, Sarmiento de Acuna (Count Gondomar), and James in turn chafed under Parliamentary pressures. James made no secret of his feelings. In 1614 he told Sarmiento, "The members (of Parliament) give their opinions in a disorderly manner. At their meetings nothing is heard but cries, shouts and confusion. I am surprised that my ancestors should ever have permitted such an institution to come into existence. I am a stranger, and found it here when I arrived, so that I am obliged to put up with what I cannot get rid of."

Catholics Under James I

The early Stuart period was a troubled time for Catholic families. Hitherto, they had not been overly concerned with the central religious conflict – that between Protestant moderates and Puritan zealots for control of the national "Anglican" Church. Yet, with the accession of James I in 1603, the Catholic question returned to the fore. James himself was anxious for a union with Rome, an ambition which united Protestant moderates and reformers alike in one goal – subjugation of the Catholics.

In his first speech to the English Parliament, James declared, "I acknowledge the Roman Church to be our Mother Church, although defiled with some infirmities and corruptions." His Protestant audience was alarmed, and took no comfort from James's statement that "my

The Gunpowder plot, Guy Fawkes with the conspirators and *right* a conspirator watched by God

mind was ever so free from persecution." Memories of the Catholic Queen Mary's persecutions still survived. However, James agreed to banish Roman Catholic priests from his kingdom, as long as they maintained the power of the Pope to depose temporal kings. But he preferred to leave ordinary Catholic people in peace, so long as they did not actively create difficulty.

It was an awkward compromise, but the King remained the sovereign power and insisted upon it. Many generations had now passed since the early movements of reform, and the severance of the English Church from the Roman by Henry VIII. A large number of Englishmen regarded the Pope, not merely as an upstart "bishop of Rome," but as the Antichrist incarnate. Catholicism was unpatriotic, and when whispers of war were in the air, no Catholic could feel entirely safe from persecution. Catholicism was identified with England's enemies, the Catholic monarchies of France and Spain.

Shortly after James ascended the throne, a national survey showed that the kingdom contained some 8,500 Catholics. The survey declared that this represented an increase over the past few years. In the year 1604 anti-Catholic legislation was strengthened, and the practice of Catholicism made a treasonable offence. Those directly affected were Jesuits, seminary priests in England, or English seminaries abroad, or any Catholic who converted an Englishman to the Roman faith. Catholics were forbidden to travel more than five miles away from their homes without first obtaining the permission of the authorities, and were heavily penalized for saying or attending masses.

Then, in 1605, occurred the Gunpowder Plot. A handful of Catholic conspirators, led by Robert Catesby, rented a cellar below the Houses of Parliament. In a carefully planned operation, barrels of gunpowder were secretly introduced into the vaults. Guido (Guy) Fawkes was the man chosen to light the fuse, when all Parliament was assembled above. But the conspirators were betrayed, and the plot discovered in time. Had it succeeded, the conspirators planned to use the confusion and disorder to seize the reins of government.

The failure of the Gunpowder Plot was the signal for renewed and

The capture of Guy Fawkes *left* and his interrogation by James I and his council

48

violent attacks on Catholic groups. More laws were passed which required Catholics not only to go through the formality of attending the services of the Church of England, but to take its sacrament. An oath was formulated, by which every subject might have to swear his allegiance to the crown, and promise to defend the crown against attack by Catholic invaders. Anyone who disobeyed these edicts was prevented from approaching to within ten miles of London, unless he was engaged in business or trade. Nor could he move farther than five miles from his home without special letters from the Privy Council itself.

How did these laws affect Catholic families in practice? Generally speaking, they were only enforced rigorously while Parliament was in session, and was able to express its collective Protestant and Puritan sentiments to the King. Between the opening of the reign in 1603 and the year 1660, only eight Catholic laymen were actually executed for recusancy, and about fifty Catholic priests also. These figures may not seem large, yet throughout England Catholic families lived in continual fear of persecution, and of antisocial conduct by extremists in the area. The Catholic became a second-class citizen, with little redress in the eyes of the law and the people.

Catholics who were executed had always had the chance to save their lives by taking the oath of allegiance, as many other Catholics had done. Indeed, one group of Catholic priests, led by George Blackwell, actually decided that this was their proper course of action. But Pope Paul V disowned them, and English Catholic priests remained split by this issue for some years. In an age without police, the law depended upon a host of disreputable informers; and these men probably did as much as any section of the community to persecute the Catholics and have them imprisoned. During James I's reign several thousand Catholic laymen and priests languished in prison with or without trial.

Charles I's Personal Rule

The marriage of Prince Charles to a French Catholic Princess, Henrietta Maria (1609–69), seemed to Parliament a foreboding of darker times. Indeed, Charles made no secret of his desire for independence. When he ascended the throne in 1625 he determined, like his father, to try and rule without the aid of the Commons. At that time, Parliament did not have a life independent of the monarchy: it could be summoned and dissolved at the King's will. The practical consideration, of course, was whether the King felt able to govern without the aid of Parliamentary funds.

Charles I's dissolutions of Parliament in 1625, 1626, and 1629 had been great disappointments to stout Protestants. *Court and Times* of March 1627/8 noted, "The House of Commons was both yesterday and today as full as one could sit by another. And they say it is the most noble, magnanimous assembly that ever these walls contained; and I heard a lord estimate they were able to buy the upper house (His Majesty only excepted) thrice over, notwithstanding there be of lords temporal to the number of 118. And what lord in England would be followed by so many freeholders as some of those are?"

Above Medallion of Henrietta Maria
Opposite: top The earliest picture of a Parliamentary session, 1624; *below left* Charles I arriving to open Parliament, *right* portrait of Charles I from a Parliamentary document

At first, Parliament directed its attacks upon the King's ministers, rather than upon the King himself. It was said that Charles was ill advised and seduced into the Catholic faith. The principal target for Parliament's attention were Charles's two chief ministers, the powerful and unpopular Archbishop William Laud (1573–1645), and Thomas Wentworth, Earl of Strafford (1593–1641).

Charles was determined to make his "divine rights" succeed in practical terms, and ruled for eleven years (1629–40) without once summoning a Parliament. Although this made the organization of opposition a difficult task, it did at the same time fire popular feeling against royal policies throughout the country. This antagonism was heightened when Charles tried to raise taxes (ship money) and customs duties (tonnage and poundage) which most people felt he could not legally impose without Parliament's consent.

Left James I welcoming his son, Charles, on his return from Spain. *Right*
A supplicant at a spiritual court, 1641

During his eleven years of personal rule, Charles tried to force his Book of Common Prayer upon the Presbyterian people of Scotland. The cry of "popery" was deafening. Robert Baillie, a moderate Scottish Presbyterian himself, was amazed at the popular fury: "What shall be the event, God knows; there was in our land ever sych an appearance of a sturr; the whole people thinks Poperie at the doores; the scandalous pamphlets which comes daily new from England, adde oyl to this flame. No man may speak any thing in publick for the King's part, except he would have himself marked for a sacrifice to be killed one day. I think our people possessed with a bloddy devill, farr above any thing that ever I could have imagined, though the masse in Latin had been presented. The minister who has the command of their mind, does disavow their unchristian humour, but are nowadays so zealous against the devill of their furie, as they are against the seducing spiriti of the bishops." By 1640 definite sides had been taken between Puritans and moderates. The moderates found themselves in what was to prove an unfortunate alliance with the Stuart monarchy.

In 1639 Charles made the Church of England prepare a statement which every clergyman throughout the land had to read in church once every three months. This statement asserted the rights of kingship in no uncertain terms. "The most high and sacred order of kings is of *divine right*, being the ordinance of God himself, founded in the prime laws of nature, and clearly established by express texts both of the Old and New Testaments. A supreme power is given to this most excellent order by God himself in the Scriptures, which is, that kings should rule and command in their several dominions all persons of what rank or estate soever. . . . For subjects to bear arms against their kings, offensive or defensive, upon any pretence whatsoever, is at least to resist the powers which are ordained of God; and . . . they shall receive to themselves damnation."

But Charles found himself unable to dispense with the services of

Archbishop William Laud

Parliament indefinitely. Now he had to pay the price. On 3rd November, 1640, his chief minister, the Earl of Strafford, was arrested for high treason. When the soldiers escorted him to prison, the crowd is said to have asked, "What's the matter?"

"A small matter, I warrant you," replied Strafford.

"Yes, indeed," shouted the spectators, "high treason is a small matter!"

At his trial, Strafford was impeached and condemned to death. There was nothing Charles could do to save him, if he was to have any hope of financial assistance from Parliament. In his heart, Charles became more determined than ever to reaffirm his sovereign power. Strafford had been a very capable administrator, and his execution a serious personal loss. Equally, having begun to taste real power, Parliament grew more determined to press home their advantage and bring the royal despot to heel.

In the meantime, the broad-based Church of England was facing mounting attack from Puritan elements. John Milton (1608–74) was one Puritan who bitterly criticized the Church in 1640–41. In a tract of June, 1641, he wrote that the clergy, through the "fraud of deceivable traditions . . . backslide one way into the Jewish beggary, and stumble forward another way into the new vomited paganism, of sensual idolatry . . . as if they could make God earthly and fleshy because they could not make themselves heavenly and spiritual." Milton condemned the high church altar as "pageanted about like a dreadful idol . . . a table of separation between priest and congregation." The bishops were scorned as yes-men of the King.

Puritans and Presbyterians alike campaigned against the sinful opulence of the bishops, and Archbishop William Laud in particular. Laud habitually travelled with forty or fifty personal attendants and ushers. "Roome, roome for my Lords Grace! Gentlemen be uncovered my Lords Grace is coming." Laud's attendants were notorious for "tumb-

Charles I touching people to cure them of illness

ling downe and thrusting aside the little children playing there: flinging and tossinge the poor costermongers and saucewives fruits and puddings, baskets and all into the Thames." Laud was destined to follow Strafford to the gallows in January 1645.

Puritans believed that the Protestant reformation had not gone far enough. The word "church" meant not a vast medieval administrative machine but a congregation of souls meeting in the presence of God, in which no distinction between the lay worshipper and a robed priest should be made. The Catholic clergy in London suffered severely from cat-calls, as one contemporary reported, "There goes a Jesuit, a Baals-priest, an Abbey-lubber, one of Canterburies whelps. . . . Divers ministers have had the surpliss torne from their backs and well they scap'd with their skins" (1640–41).

These were uncertain times for ordinary people. On the one hand were the Catholic families, who could not in conscience accept the Protestant church, with its denials of Catholic beliefs, loyalties, and forms of worship. On the other hand were the reforming Puritans, whose methods, often violent and extreme, were nevertheless inspired by a deep loyalty to the Scriptures. Both sides regarded themselves as missionaries. The Puritans wished to impose their rules on every English family; Catholic factions continually sought the ear of the sympathetic Stuart kings, and Jesuit priests journeyed secretly about the country to rally the support of the leading Catholic families. Many good middle-of-the-road Protestants wished to see the end of all extremism and persecution. But in an age of deep religious convictions, Catholics and Puritans alike believed it was better to burn at the stake than to risk eternal damnation by swearing oaths against their conscience.

In 1642 Puritan extremists united in an attack on kingship, which was based on the exclusive privileges of the Church. In a pamphlet, *Spirituall Snapsacks for the Parliament Soldiers*, they wrote: "Consider the

A cartoon against lax non-resident priests, 1642

parties against whom you fight are a most idolatrous, superstitious, delinquent, prophane, ignorant, or hypocriticall generation, take them where you will, from one degree to another, and you may fitly ranke them under some of those unworthy denominations; for either they are Papists and so idolatrous; praelaticall, and so superstitious; offenders of several kinds and so delinquents; men of cursing, deboist [debauch], lips and lies, and so profane."

This was the language of civil war.

Poverty of Clergy

Unfortunately, the Church of England was poorly equipped to deal with the crisis. The links between the rich and influential upper clergy (the bishops) and the parish clergy were tenuous; most parish priests not only lacked recognition, but faced a hard struggle for a bare existence; most lacked the education or understanding to help create a religious settlement.

Tudor England had grown steadily richer, yet when James Stuart ascended the English throne in 1603, the lower clergy still remained an underpaid, underprivileged section of the community. Archbishop John Whitgift (1530–1604) had declared that half of the nine thousand benefices carried incomes of under £10, often much less. Most incumbents had no university degree, and less than half were actually licensed to preach. The only way a priest could supplement his income was to neglect his pastoral duties and take a post as chaplain to a wealthy family, or hold more than one benefice at a time. Neither solution helped the Church. However, a closer attention to Church law, especially concerning its land, at least helped to check the despoiling of its wealth by those court favourites who wielded ecclesiastical patronage. Nor was church-going universal. Many a priest wrote tracts or pamphlets bemoaning low attendances and uncivilized conduct in church. Yet the religious opinions and prejudices of most parishioners were strongly held.

Schooling

As the century progressed increasing importance was attached to education by all but the very poorest classes. James Howell wrote in 1647, "Every man strains his fortunes to keep his children at school. The cobbler will clout it till midnight, the porter will carry burdens till his bones crack again, the ploughman will pinch both back and belly to give his son learning, and I find that this ambition reigns nowhere so much as in this island." Many people saw education as a way of gaining religious knowledge, and therefore as a highly desirable pursuit. Learning, even in its most elementary form, was firmly based on religion. One alphabet, popular at the time, began:

> In Adam's fall
> We sinned all,

and ended:

> Zaccheus he
> Did climb a tree
> Our Lord to see.

This emphasis on religion had the undoubted disadvantage that it restricted learning. In the lower forms of education this did not really matter, but in the grammar schools little attention was paid to mathematics and the growing subject of science. Most importance was attached to classical subjects – Latin, Greek, logic, rhetoric, and some Hebrew – all of which would help the pupil understand religious matters and theological writings and disputations.

Because childhood at this time was so short, education naturally started early, and children often received their first simple lessons when only two years old. Regular lessons probably started when a child was about four, with its nurse or mother as the teacher. The textbook for these first lessons was a "horn-book", a piece of wood shaped like a paddle on which was pasted a printed page showing the alphabet, the Lord's Prayer, and numbers. Over this was a piece of transparent horn held in place by a brass binding. A quill or straw fescue, for the teacher to point out what was to be learned, was included in the purchase price of threepence.

The early home schooling of the sons of yeomen and lesser gentry was followed by attendance at the village dame's school, or perhaps a school founded by an itinerant schoolmaster, who had decided to stop awhile in the village. Many schoolmasters were devout Puritans. Under their guidance, religion, reading, writing, and arithmetic were (often inadequately) taught. What little learning a man did receive seems to have been soon forgotten, and adults had small opportunity to practise these laboriously acquired arts; it was never regarded as a disgrace if one could not write. From wills of the period it would seem that between sixty and seventy per cent of the yeoman class could write their names; for many this was the sum of their achievement.

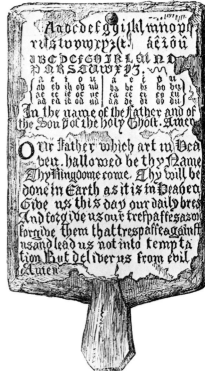

A "horn-book", a child's first textbook

A master with his class in the early years of the century

After the small schools came the grammar or Latin schools. Here the teaching was classical with, as always, religion. The rod with which pupils were beaten was an ever present reminder of the biblical virtues of discipline and obedience for girls and boys alike.

The grammar schools accepted pupils from all backgrounds, whether sons of squires, small nobility, clergy, yeomen, or intelligent village boys. The seventeenth century was the heyday of the grammar school. In the first half of the century more new schools were privately endowed than in the whole of the previous century. The statutes often embodied the religious preferences of the founder. The pupils of these schools were certainly intended to work hard. In summer, morning lessons began at six o'clock and ended at eleven, and afternoon school lasted from one o'clock until six. In winter, as a concession to the long dark days, the school day began an hour later and ended an hour earlier. John Brinsley, an authority on education, advocated in *A Consolation for Our Grammar Schools* (1622) that, once a week, children should have part of the afternoon free for recreation; but few masters were so enlightened.

The sons of the wealthy generally studied at home with private tutors. Girls born into these households were lucky, as they could learn on an equal footing with their brothers. Among the wealthy, at least, female learning was not then frowned upon. John Milton's daughters, for example, could read and speak six languages, and although this was exceptional, most women could speak two or three; Puritans might learn German, and Catholics French and Spanish. Some families sent their daughters to boarding schools; a popular one was started at this time in Hackney, but the shortage of such schools limited the number who could do this. When anti-Catholic feeling ran high, Catholic families preferred to send their children to be educated abroad in a Catholic country, such as France, Italy, or Spain. Few girls had the chance of having eight tutors to teach her, as had Lucy Apsley. The great majority had little education once the horn-book had been outgrown, except to prepare them for managing a home and family.

During the century it became common to send boys to schools beyond the nearest grammar school. Among the most popular of these were Eton, Westminister – best known for its classical education and Royalist sympathies – Winchester ("the best nursery for learning for young children in the world"), and St. Paul's, where John Milton, Samuel Pepys, and John Churchill were educated. The newer foundations, begun just before the start of the century, included Rugby, Uppingham, and Merchant Taylor's. All these schools are still flourishing today.

One, begun in 1590, came to achieve fame beyond its founder's dreams. This was Harrow School, started by a childless yeoman farmer, John Lyon, so that the poorer local boys might have an education, if they were clever enough. The statutes of the school provided for archery practice, physical exercise, and service to the state, "each child to furnish his own bowshafts and bowstrings" as well as his own writing materials, "and candles for the winter." However, if there were not enough local boys to fill the places the master could admit "foreigners" from outside the village of Harrow. Out of this small village charity grew one of England's most famous public schools.

Opposite Oliver Cromwell, leader of the militant opposition to Charles I, was Lord Protector of England from 1649 to his death in 1658. Portrait by R. Walker, *c.* 1649

Opposite Charles II, eldest son of the deposed Charles I, was invited to return to the English throne by Parliament in 1660. This undated portrait is from the studio of J. M. Wright. *Left* Nell Gwyn, Charles's favourite mistress, *c.* 1675. *Below* Catherine of Braganza Princess of Portugal and Queen of Charles II, portrait by D. Stoop, *c.* 1660–61

The Great Fire of London, 1666. St. Paul's Cathedral is in flames, the houses at the end of London Bridge are nearly destroyed and on the right the Tower of London is illuminated by the flames

"Prospect of London and the Thames from above Greenwich," painted *c.* 1620–30: this is the earliest known painting of a view of London from a distance. St. Paul's is seen faintly in the distance on the left and on the right is Greenwich Palace and the little village of Deptford

3 Cavaliers and Roundheads

THE YEAR 1640 was a crucial one for the future of England. In this year, threatened by an armed Scottish rebellion against his despotic religious policies, Charles I had no choice but to summon an English Parliament. Only Parliament could provide him with enough money to crush the Scots. But the Short Parliament, as it was called, was not prepared to finance Charles on the terms he proposed, and within three weeks Charles announced its dissolution.

But as Charles was threatened with real bankruptcy he had no choice but to summon another Parliament. That which met in November 1640 was known as the Long Parliament, and among its leaders was a Somerset squire, the Puritan reformer John Pym (1584–1643). In view of the King's imminent bankruptcy, the Long Parliament was able to drive the hardest bargain of Charles's reign. The King's chief ministers, Archbishop William Laud and the Earl of Strafford were both dismissed from office; Strafford was executed the following May (1641); the Star Chamber Court through which Charles had enforced his despotism was abolished; a Triennial Act was passed to ensure that Parliaments were called at regular three-year intervals, instead of at the King's pleasure; monopolies were abolished; and Charles's taxes (ship money, tonnage, and poundage) declared unconstitutional.

John Pym, the Puritan reformer who led the anti-Charles faction in the Long Parliament

Further sweeping reforms were proposed in Parliament's Grand Remonstrance, produced by John Pym, but not every Member of Parliament would support it. Was this Charles's opportunity to retrieve his position? If it was, he characteristically threw it away. On 4th January, 1642, he personally entered the House of Commons to arrest John Pym and four other Members. Brushing aside, as it did, ancient Parliamentary privilege, this was an act of sheer folly. In fact, Pym and the others had already escaped, but the damage was done. It was now clear beyond doubt that Charles had not the slightest intention of bargaining with Parliament. A King who considered himself to stand so high above the law was not, in Parliament's eyes, fit to rule.

A cartoon of 1641 showing religion, the Bible, being tossed about by the various sects

In the spring of 1642 both Parliament and the King began to prepare for war. Parliament took steps to raise an army of ten thousand men, and Charles moved his court out of London to the city of Nottingham. For the next three years, there were in effect two governments in England: the revolutionary Parliament in London, drawing most of its

Opposite James Edward Stuart, the Old Pretender, as a child with his sister, Louisa Maria Teresa, painted by M. de Lagillière *c.* 1695

The trial *left* and execution *right* of Thomas, Earl of Strafford and Lord Lieutenant of Ireland in 1641

The Roundhead, a popular weapon

The Royal Standard raised at Nottingham

Omens said to predict the troubled times

support from London and the east of England; and the King, drawing most support from the north and west. But this was primarily a war fought for ideas and principles, not for territorial conquest. Rebel Members of Parliament, Puritans throughout the country, and merchants who had refused to pay Charles's unconstitutional taxes – these formed the nucleus of the Roundheads dominated by the soldier-statesman Oliver Cromwell. Catholics, Royalists, conservatives and many moderates formed the nucleus of the Royalists or Cavaliers. Often these divisions cut across family ties, and caused a bitterness and hatred which was to linger on for many years in English society.

From Monarchy to Republic

After fighting had broken out in August, 1642, Oliver Cromwell quickly became the most prominent soldier on the Parliamentary side. A devout Puritan and fine cavalry officer, he set about reorganizing the Parliamentary forces, and created what became known as the New Model Army. The New Model Army quickly won success, and under Thomas Fairfax (1611–71) gained their first great victory over King Charles at the battle of Naseby in Northamptonshire, on 14th June, 1645. Charles fled the battlefield, and gave himself up to the Scots, with whom he at once began to negotiate.

In London, some Members of Parliament, mainly Presbyterians, wanted to end the war and negotiate a proper settlement with the defeated King. But others (called Independents) angrily disagreed. These included Cromwell himself. On 6th December, 1648, a detachment of the New Model Army under Colonel Thomas Pride invaded the House of Commons and turned the Presbyterians out. Pride's purge left Parliament with some fifty Members. The fifty-strong Rump Parliament, as it became known, now proclaimed that Charles Stuart was a traitor to his people, and must be put on trial for high treason. On 27th January, 1649, the captive King whom the Scots had given over to the English, was found guilty of being a "tyrant, traitor, murderer and public enemy of the good people of England," and three days later was beheaded on a scaffold outside Whitehall Palace in London.

England was now a republic, or to use a seventeenth-century term, commonwealth. The monarchy and the House of Lords were formally

Left The members of the House of Commons being expelled by Cromwell, 1648. *Right* The execution of Archbishop Laud in 1641

abolished. Within four years, however, Cromwell and the New Model Army fell into bitter dispute with the Rump Parliament, about the latter's excessive constitutional powers (the Rump was a supreme law-making body, and could perpetuate its own life indefinitely). Once again, Parliament was purged by the Army, but this time completely. It is said that someone wrote on the door of St. Stephen's Chapel, where the Rump had met, "This house is to let. Now unfurnished." After a short interval of government by a Provisional Council, supreme executive power was vested in a Lord Protector and Council. Oliver Cromwell became Lord Protector, and dominated the Protectorate from this time (1653) until his death on 3rd September, 1658. By that time, the Roundhead side was torn with disputes between soldiers and Parliamentarians, and between Puritans, Independents, Presbyterians, and other religious sects, and plans were soon begun to invite Charles I's son (Charles II) to take back his throne. This was the tense and complex background to English life for a generation, until the Restoration of Charles II in 1660.

Playing card satirizing the Rump Parliament

London during the Civil Wars

In 1642 Parliament was preparing to defend London by force against the King who was then encamped at Oxford. Thirty years before, the Lord Mayor had fixed the city militia at 6,000 men, and this was now the nucleus of the capital's defence. City companies like the Armourers and the Cutlers provided firearms, weapons, and other military equipment.

In February, 1643, with the Royalist army menacing London, the Common Council took further steps for city defence. They erected small forts at strategic points by the city outskirts, with batteries, redoubts, and ditches in support. The entrances to certain streets were hurriedly bricked up – including part of St. James, Holborn, and St. John Street in the east end – and turnpikes put up in other places. A contemporary historian, James Sharpe, doubted whether the city militia would be a powerful enough defence. He agreed that the militia were efficient but pointed out that a much larger permanent force was needed, and that the voluntary service of local shopkeepers and tradesmen could not be relied upon indefinitely. But the money needed to field a larger army remained a basic problem for the Parliamentary leaders.

Fear and panic were widespread, and after 1642 many innocent people were arrested. The historian James Howell (1594–1666) was one. One morning, he wrote, five armed men with swords and pistols broke into his chamber saying they had a Parliamentary warrant for his arrest, but they would not show it to him. The soldiers ransacked his house and seized a large number of papers. When they left, two guards remained behind on watch until the time of Howell's examination. When at last he was examined by the Close Committee, nothing could be proved against him, but he was nevertheless marched off to the Fleet Prison. Howell wrote: "I must lie dead at anchor in this Fleet a long time, unless some gentle gale blow thence to make me launch out."

Left Isaac Pennington, Lord Mayor of London at the start of the war in 1643. *Centre* Roundhead propaganda print showing cruelties said to be committed by the Cavaliers. *Right* Firing a cannon

A pikeman

The historian Sir William Dugdale (1605–86) recorded two similar cases. The first occurred in the village of Acton, six miles outside London, where "a sober, moderate and charitable minded man" was attacked, for "difference in religion." A unit of Parliamentary soldiers invaded his house, auctioned off all his furniture there and then, and sent his servants on foot to London; and for good measure they dug up every tree and shrub in his orchard. The other case involved a man aged over eighty who was assaulted by soldiers billeted in houses near by. Using the excuse of a forged document, they entered his house and tore it apart, "leaving him nothing but naked walls and one stoole, which the old man sate upon, he being lame and decrepit with old age." In these perilous times, no one guilty of "difference in religion" could feel that his person and property were safe.

The way in which Puritanism affected ordinary life during the Civil Wars is shown in this extract from the parish records of St. Giles in London. Most of the fines listed below concerned offences against the Sabbath:

1641   Received of the Vintner at the Catt in Queen Street for permitting of tipling on the Lord's Day   £1   10   0
1644   Received of three poore men, for drinking on the Sabbath daie at Tottenham Court   4   0

1645	Received of John Seagood, constable, which he had of Frenchman for swearing three oathes	3	0
1645	Received of Mrs. Thunder, by the hands of Francis Potter for her being drunk and swearing seaven oaths	12	0
1646	Received of Mr. Hooker for brewing on a Fast day	2	6
	Received of four men, travelling on the Fast day	1	0
1646	Received of Mr. Wetherill, headboro', which he had of one for an oath	3	4
1648	Received from the Citty Marshall, sent by the Lord Mayor, for one that was drunke at the Forts in our parish	5	0
	Received from Isabel Johnson at ye Coleyard for drinking on the Sabbath day	4	0
1652	Received of Mr. Huxley and Mr. Morris, who were riding out of town in sermon time on a Fast day	11	0

Left Jock the Scotsman presenting a petition to the king complaining of the disturbances caused by the Civil War in Scotland in 1648. *Centre* Prince Rupert, general of the king's cavalry. *Right* Two militiamen

1654	Received of William Glover in Queen Street, and of Isaac Thomas a barber in Holborn, for trimming a beard on the Lord's day	*sum omitted*	
1655	Received of Mayde taken in Mrs. Jackson's ale-house on the Sabbath day	5	0
	Received of a Scotchman drinking at Robert Owne's on the Sabbath	2	0
1658	Received of Joseph Piers for refusing to open his doores to have his house searched on the Lord's daie	10	0

A Roundhead cavalryman

Petty criminals suffered terribly during the Protectorate. Puritan magistrates were stern and unrelenting, as the case of one Francis Prideaux shows. Convicted of taking away lead from the home of one Richard Rothwell he was fined a shilling, and publicly whipped at the cart tail for two hours "until his body be bloddy," and then committed to the Gatehouse Prison until the fine had been paid together with costs of three shillings and eightpence.

Samuel Pepys (1632–1703) was a young boy living in London when the Civil Wars began, and his family – like so many others – was split by events. One of his uncles, Apollo, was a diehard Royalist, and was lodged in the Tower of London for refusing to swear an oath of Parliamentary loyalty; but another uncle, Robert Pepys of Brampton, became a captain in the Parliamentary militia. Samuel's own parents were devout Puritans, and had no doubt which side deserved their support, and Samuel grew up as enthusiastic as many other members of the younger generation for reform. Perhaps more by accident than design, he fell passionately in love with a French girl, Elizabeth, herself the daughter of French Huguenot (Protestant) parents, and married her on 10th October, 1655. Pepys became closely concerned with the stern and efficient Cromwellian administration at Whitehall, when he began to work for his elder cousin Montague. Yet, like many of his contemporaries who reached adulthood in the 1650s and 1660s, Pepys' youthful loyalties changed with the restoration of Charles II, and he became as strong a court man as any of his friends, and more so than some.

As the years passed, the people of London rose in anger against the harsh methods used to raise funds for the army. Mrs. Lucy Hutchinson, the wife of a colonel in the New Model Army, recalled how guards came to her house to collect taxes, and how – when she asked their authority – more than fifty men overran her house and made off with over £25 as well as the tax money, insulted her and spat in her face. With incidents like these multiplied every day, feeling ran so high in the City that Parliamentary soldiers grew afraid to walk the streets in uniform for fear of being violently attacked and reviled. When at last the City of London refused to pay any more taxes to the Parliament, a force was sent in to tear down the city gates and seize eleven leading citizens as hostages.

Had the Civil Wars come to this, that a struggle for liberty against the King had degenerated in a struggle for liberty by the common people against their own Parliament?

Disruption of Family Life

Through these years of complex military activity, and religious strife, one of the saddest aspects was the separation of families. Husbands and sons rode away to fight, and mothers and young children were left behind to defend their homes as best they could, praying that the Roundhead (Parliamentary) and Cavalier (Royalist) armies would leave them in peace. Some families, like the Verneys, sought refuge in remote corners of the country, or went into voluntary exile abroad. Every carrier, coach driver, or other person making his way through the countryside was anxiously pressed for news of the movement of troops under Oliver Cromwell and Sir Thomas Fairfax, or under King Charles and Prince Rupert (1619–82).

Family records of this period often refer to the bravery of wives who defended their homes against the enemy in the absence of their menfolk. One of the most remarkable cases was that of Charlotte de la Tremouille, Countess of Derby. James, the Earl of Derby, was himself away fighting under the Royalist banner. In May, 1643, the Roundhead Governor of Manchester called upon Charlotte to surrender the Derby home, Lathom House in Lancashire. The story of the dramatic two-year siege which followed was set down by one of the soldiers employed by Charlotte, Captain Edward Halsall. Halsall wrote: "She (Charlotte)

Above James Stanley, Earl of Derby and *below* his wife Charlotte

endured a continued siege, being with the exception of her gardens and walks, confined as a prisoner within her own walls, with the liberty of the castle yard, suffering the sequestration of her whole estate, besides daily affronts and indignities from unworthy persons, and the unjust and undeserved censures of some that wore the name and face of friends; all of which she patiently endured, well knowing it to be no wisdom to quarrel with an evil she could not redress." Sieges of great residences like Lathom House became a common feature of the Civil Wars.

With three hundred Cavalier soldiers and several pieces of artillery under her command, the brave Countess held out for two years against her besiegers. On 29th May, 1645, the siege was raised by the arrival of an army under Prince Rupert himself, who "this day not only relieved but revenged the most noble lady his cousin," by presenting her with twenty-two of the military standards that a few days before had defiantly flown before her gates. Charlotte now withdrew to the Isle of Man, owned by the Derby family, and left the defence of Lathom House to Colonel Rawsthorne. When at last the house fell to Round-head troops in 1645, even the Roundheads admitted that Charlotte had proved "herself the better soldier of the two."

A sketch of Prince Rupert in 1644

But in the years after the trial and execution of Charles I (1649) tragedy befell the Derby family. Lord Derby himself was captured and killed at Bolton-le-Moors on 15th October, 1651, and two of Charlotte's children died in prison of smallpox. Charlotte herself was betrayed by a friend and thrown into prison; she lived to return to Lathom House after the Restoration, and resided there quietly until her death in 1663.

Secret hiding places and "priest holes" may seem romantic today, but during the Civil Wars they served a very important purpose, especially for Catholic families who retained their own priest in defiance of the law. These hiding places came in useful on many occasions, even for non-Catholics, or for anyone who sought to escape capture. One Royalist, Arthur Jones, who fought beside the disinherited Charles II at his resounding defeat at Worcester in 1651, escaped to his home, Chastleton House, in Oxfordshire, closely pursued by a Cromwellian detachment. He arrived a few minutes before his hunters and his wife hid him in a secret room, the Cavalier Room, built in the house by his grandfather Walter Jones in the time of James I. The soldiers stormed into the house and ransacked it from top to bottom, but could find nothing. Mrs. Jones, anxious not to arouse their suspicions, offered them wine and hospitality; but she took care to drug the wine. After an hour the soldiers fell unconscious, and Mrs. Jones was able to help her husband escape on one of the officers' horses.

Sir Kenelm Digby, a Royalist Catholic, duelling in 1641

A vivid record of the Civil Wars is contained in the pages of an account book kept by one Mrs. Jefferies, who lived in Widemarsh Street, Hereford, and owned several other local properties. She wrote her first entries in 1638, one of which noted the payment of the hated and unconstitutional ship money to the King. The account book lists a number of other smaller payments to various persons, apparently meant to reduce trouble. In September, 1639, Mrs. Jefferies paid two shillings to "a strange soldier with a blue feather in his hat who said he came from Berwick," and in October, fourpence to "a counterfeit soldier, or a thief rather." She also contributed toward the defence of Hereford. In 1638 she paid five shillings to the city trained bands (militia), and in 1640 another two shillings to a man "watching one night at Widemarsh Gate." Two years later she was frightened by the explosion of muskets outside her house, but managed to pacify the strangers by some timely hospitality: "The soldiers that shot off at my window, one shilling and beer."

War rapidly overtook the city of Hereford, and from 1642 to 1644 her house was billeted by noisy Roundhead soldiers. Mrs. Jefferies herself had packed her personal belongings and fled to seek refuge with friends. In 1644 Royalist forces under Prince Rupert drove out the Parliamentarians, and Mrs. Jefferies returned home; but in 1645, with Hereford again in danger, her houses and many other properties in the suburbs were demolished to make way for the defence of the city. One of her houses had only recently been built at a cost of £800, and she herself had not crossed the threshold before the militia pulled it down. A Hereford soldier, Sir Henry Slingsby, who kept a diary of these events, deeply mourned the great sacrifices which the city people had been forced to make. He remembered how one woman who (like Mrs. Jefferies) had lost her house, later died of grief. But the sacrifices were rewarded: the invading army of 2,500 men under General Leslie was driven away after an exhausting siege of five weeks.

Sometimes, ordinary men and women could suddenly be caught up in high adventures, many of which became legendary. A girl called Jane Lane who lived in Bentley, Staffordshire, was asked to ride south with her cousin Henry Lascelles to Abbot's Leigh near Bristol. The cousins were attended on their journey by a serving man in a grey suit and tall black hat, named William Jackson. No one else guessed that Jackson was really Charles Stuart fleeing his realm with a price of £1,000 on his royal head. After an anxious eight-day ride over muddy roads, the party reached Abbot's Leigh, where a startled butler recognized the future Charles II. Luckily the butler was a devout Royalist, and held his tongue. After many difficulties a small boat was found to take Charles across the Channel from Bristol to France, where he landed on 16th October, 1651. When Jane's part in the plot was discovered, she too was forced into exile in France.

A similar adventure befell Anne Murray (later Lady Halkett), who helped the fourteen-year-old heir apparent, the Duke of York, escape from St. James Palace to France on 20th April, 1648, a year before his father's execution. Anne's task was to obtain some clothes so that the Duke could be disguised as a girl. She measured the boy and went to a London tailor to have the clothes made. In her *Autobiography* she remembered how surprised the tailor had been at the list of measurements. He said "he had made many gowns and suits, but he had never made any to such a person in his life . . . he had never seen any woman of so low a stature have so big a waist." However, the tailor did what was required, and the clothes were delivered, "a mixed mohair of a light hair colour and black, and ye under-petticoat was scarlet."

After a few more days' anxious preparation: "His Highness called,

Charles II and Jane Lane passing through a Roundhead troop

'Quickly, quickly, dress me,' and putting off his clothes, I dressed him in the woman's habit that was prepared, which fitted his Highness very well, and was very pretty in it." Then after a quick meal, Colonel Bamfield who was in charge of the arrangements took his charge down to the river steps: the "girl" slipped away on a barge down the Thames, and arrived at Gravesend, where a boat was waiting to leave for France. As Cromwell extended his power over the country, and Parliamentary spies and informers were everywhere, such exploits were attended with great risks.

Woodcut from the *Kingdomes Weekly Post*, a journal of the time, 1644

During the Protectorate many Royalist noblemen and gentry lost their property. As the military conquest proceeded after the Royalist defeats at Naseby (1645) and Worcester (1651), Parliament exacted fines upon Royalist properties equal to anything between a tenth and a third of their value. Many of the victims were forced to sell their estates to raise cash. Coupled with the total confiscation and resale of the property of about seventy leading Royalists in 1651, this created a glut on the property market, with the result that the hardship upon the Royalists was even greater. Many fled the country, their families and fortunes forever ruined.

But despite every setback, most Royalists never dreamed of deserting their cause; they were dedicated to avenging the memory of their murdered King. Edward Hyde (later the first Earl of Clarendon) (1608–74) addressed these brave words to fellow Royalists: "We must play out the game with that courage as becomes gamesters, who were first engaged by conscience against all motives of temptation and interest, and to be glad to let the world know that we carried on only by conscience."

It is not known exactly how much property changed hands during the Protectorate, but it was certainly a good deal, and the changes were in many cases destined to be permanent. Many Royalists had been forced to dispose of their lands "voluntarily" to pay the enormous fines, and so had no legal redress after the Restoration. Only those whose property had been confiscated were able to recover it.

Who took the place of the expropriated Royalists? The "new gentry", as they were called, usually came either from the richer merchant class, or from the military. A satirist of 1647 lamented:

I now have lived to see the day,
Wherein a fig-man bears such sway,
  That knights dare scarce sit by him;
Yea, I have lived to see the hour,
In which a clothier hath such power,
  That lords are glad to buy him.

Thus do the froth of all the earth,
A spawn sprung from a dunghill birth,
  Now prince it in our land:
A people come the Lord knows how,
Both fame and nameless till just now,
  Must every one command.

The new gentry included, for example, those who had mortgaged

Royalist property to help raise fines, and later took possession of that property. They included those who had supported Cromwell with money or influence, and were rewarded with confiscated lands. Many leading Roundhead officers were paid off with Royalist estates, and now assumed leading social positions in county life. Charles Fleetwood, for example, took Woodstock Manor, John Lambert took Wimbledon, John Okey went to Ampthill in Bedfordshire, and Thomas Pride took the great palace of Nonesuch (see illustration pages 34–35). In these ways, the Commonwealth represented not only a political revolution, but something of a social revolution as well.

The Civil Wars and Religious Life

Many people tried to lead quiet and normal lives during the Civil Wars, but no one remained untouched by changes in the religious framework. After 1652 wedding ceremonies had to be conducted by magistrates rather than priests, and the whole character of weddings changed until the Restoration of 1660. The magistrate might simply hold in his hand the Puritan Directory, the substitute for the old Prayer Book, and ask the couple to declare their wish to marry in front of witnesses. He then pronounced a simple formula, and they became man and wife. Many Protestants felt this to be a very inadequate ceremony. When Lady Anne Halkett, for example, had gone through the Puritan form of marriage, she had her marriage confirmed in church. She said, "If it had not been done more solemnly afterwards by a minister I should not have believed it lawfully done." Needless to say, the light-hearted wedding-day festivities with their drinking and dancing came to a stop during the Commonwealth, and were only brought back with the Restoration of Charles II.

The Prayer Book had been full of rules offensive to the zealous Puritan – for example, the making of the sign of the cross at baptism, and the custom of kneeling for Holy Communion. During the Civil Wars the Prayer Book was replaced by the Directory, a shorter and more severe form of service. Episcopacy was abolished and a new organization based upon Presbyterian congregations was set up. Elders of the London congregation met for the first time in 1646. This at least was the bones of the new order. It is difficult to assess how far it was adopted in practice. In an age of poor road communications, it is likely that many a village and hamlet persisted in its old forms of worship in defiance, or even ignorance, of the new measures.

A special feature of the first half of the century was the great flood of devotional books which came on to the market, and which encouraged independence of priests and formal church doctrine. People were encouraged to spend their time in private prayer and enter into direct communication with God. One of the most prominent new sects to arise during the Civil Wars was the Quakers, inspired by George Fox (1624–90) whom many regarded as the prophet of a new world. Other sects included John Lilburne's (1618–57) Levellers (with a strongly political basis), and Gerrard Winstanley's Diggers (with a primitive communist outlook).

John Lilburne, leader of the Levellers sect

Those families who clung to the old worship of the Church of England were unwilling witnesses to many changes in their parishes. Under a Puritan law of 1643, local committees were set up throughout the country to purge the clergy, as a result of which one parish in three found itself with a new priest. Many of the ejected clergy fled the country; some were imprisoned; and those with large families often faced a real threat of starvation. Most of their places were taken by Presbyterians or Independents, who brought with them styles of worship often unfamiliar and objectionable to local families.

Many Royalist priests preferred to cut their cloth according to the times. Many of them had large families to support, and on their meagre income dared not offend the current demands of the authorities. The classic example in literature of such a priest was the Vicar of Bray:

> In good King Charles's golden days,
> When loyalty no harm meant;
> A furious high churchman I was,
> And so I gained preferment.
> Unto my flock I daily preached,
> Kings are by God appointed,
> And damned are those who dare resist
> Or touch the Lord's Anointed.
> And this is law, I will maintain,
> Unto my dying day, Sir,
> That whatsoever king shall reign,
> I will be the Vicar of Bray, Sir!

At great risk to themselves, some Royalist families began to hold daily services in their own homes, under the old customs. Their safety depended on the knowledge or connivance of other local residents, who in their own zeal might often betray them to the authorities.

The diarist John Evelyn (1620–1706), however, found at least one church in London in 1655 where the Stuart liturgy remained in use, St. Gregory's, although the incumbent John Hewitt was executed for conspiracy in 1658. Elsewhere, the churches were occupied by Presbyterians or Independents. Once, Evelyn was astonished to see an ignorant mechanic climb into the pulpit, shouting that the saints were calling men to destroy earthly government, and other "such feculent stuff."

Births and burials, too, were affected by the new order in an ordinance of 24th August, 1653. The old Anglican services gave way to a simple civilian registration for a fourpenny fee. Those who wished to have traditional baptisms or burials had to ask sympathizers for an Anglican priest willing to risk the heavy penalties involved. The body of Charles I itself was swiftly buried according to the form of the Directory, although John Evelyn managed to procure a traditional burial service for his mother-in-law, the first in that particular church building for seven years. Evelyn wailed, "The Lord Jesus pity our distressed church, and bring back the captivity of Zion!"

Writing after the Restoration, the Earl of Clarendon (Edward Hyde) considered that the wars had had a bad effect on the younger generation. Children, he said, did not seek the blessing of their parents; they conversed without any circumspection or modesty, and often met at

John Evelyn who recorded the troubled times in his Diary

taverns and common eating houses; daughters of noble families had no shame in marrying divines (preachers) below their social rank; parents lost their authority over their children. Ending on a high note, Clarendon declared, "There were never such examples of impiety between such relations in any age of the world, Christian or heathen, as that wicked time, from the beginning of the rebellion to the King's return." Clarendon perhaps allowed his feelings to take control of his reason.

After Charles I had dissolved Parliament in 1629, the Roman Catholics enjoyed a period of renewed freedom from persecution. Queen Henrietta Maria (1609–69) led a considerable Catholic court party, and masses were regularly celebrated in her chapel. But with the summoning of what was to be known as the Long Parliament, this time passed. Protestantism recovered its voice, fired incidentally by a Catholic rebellion in Ireland, and the Catholic issue became a dominant one in the negotiations between Parliament and King which immediately preceded the outbreak of hostilities.

After the First Civil War had begun in 1642, Catholic families began to suffer. Records of September, 1655, show that nearly 1,600 Catholics had had their property seized, and were left only a small portion for the support of their wives and children. Even this small portion was allowed only if the mother undertook to raise her children as good Protestants. Catholics suffered, too, from punitive taxation, and from seizure of their horses and arms. In 1643 the Long Parliament drafted an oath specially designed to ferret out Catholics. The oath was a renunciation of Papal supremacy, transubstantiation, purgatory, and other Catholic beliefs, in short an impossible test for any good Catholic. As a result, many hundreds were caught and severely penalized. In the 1650s anti-Catholic pressure was eased a little, but attendance and celebration of mass was still forbidden. One possible solution, taken up by many of the Catholic gentry, was to move to London, where they could worship at the private Catholic chapels of various foreign diplomats recognized and protected by Cromwell.

Dr. Thomas Fuller

Out of the harsh and unjust experiences of the mid-seventeenth century, however, grew a freer religious atmosphere, which was to provide a basis for toleration in England in later generations. Perhaps this was because so many religious voices had been making themselves heard – Catholics, Puritans, Quakers, Baptists and Anabaptists, Independents, Armenians, Jews, Levellers, Diggers, and others. Despite cruelty and bigotry by many individuals, mainly in the Puritan arena, the Commonwealth by and large justified Cromwell's boast that "I meddle not with any man's conscience." A leading Puritan, the poet John Milton (1608–74), believed that persecution was in any case unnecessary, because in the end the truth was its own best safeguard. "Rigid external formality" and "gross conforming stupidity" were not the way to ensure the truth and righteousness of religion.

The life of Dr. Thomas Fuller (1608–61), author of *The History of the Worthies of England* (published 1662), shows some of the complexities of opinion during the Civil Wars. Fuller himself was, if asked, a supporter of the Royalist cause; and yet during the reign of Charles I he had

The many varieties of religious beliefs and practices shown in a print of
1644

spoken strongly against the policies of Charles's minister, Archbishop William Laud. Fuller saw nothing inconsistent in this, although such distinctions were often drowned in the popular roar for "Reform."

During the years of crisis Fuller (who was then a priest) married, a common enough event. But as his new brother-in-law, Captain Hugh Grove, was a Royalist hero, Fuller thought it prudent to conceal news of the marriage from Puritan officials for as long as possible. Indeed, despite Fuller's extensive writings and diaries, historians did not discover the fact of the marriage until as late as 1918.

Like many of his contemporaries, Fuller believed in moderation – not in the sense of compromise or evasion, but as "a mixture of discretion and charity in one's judgement . . . pride is the greatest enemy to moderation," he added, thinking no doubt of extreme Puritans and Papists alike, "Proud men having studied some additional point in Divinity will strive to make the same necessary to Salvation, to enhance the value of their own worth and pains."

Preaching in London in 1642, when Parliament had already begun to garrison London against the King, Fuller declared: "Think not that the King's army is like Sodom . . . and the other army like Zion . . . no, there be drunkards on both sides, and swearers on both sides, and profane on both sides."

The purge of Royalist priests which took place in London during 1642 left Fuller as virtually the last King's man still with a pulpit. Parliament may have wanted to use Fuller as a go-between, negotiating between London and Oxford, where the King had his court. Fuller himself was very distressed: "Must the new foe quite jostle out the old friend?" Many good men like Fuller found themselves in the crossfire between the armed combatants; it was a situation which was to cause prolonged and genuine hardship for all those who wanted church reform, but at the same time kept to their oaths of allegiance to the King. It was the tragedy of mid-seventeenth-century England that their voices were drowned. Thomas Fuller himself saw no practical alternative but to swear the new Parliamentary oath: "I will not consent to the laying down of arms so long as the Papists, now in open war against the Parliament, shall by force of arms be protected from the justice thereof: I will not, directly or indirectly, adhere unto, nor shall willingly assist the forces raised by the King without the consent of both Houses of Parliament."

But Fuller knew that in practice he could not support such a policy. It reversed every hope that he cherished for national unity. His last act before leaving London was to publish his *Sermon of Reformation*, in which he bitterly attacked the disruptive work of the Assembly of Divines in London. Then he left to join the King's court at Oxford.

Caught up in the years of military action which followed, Thomas Fuller mournfully wrote, "For the first five years, during our actual Civil Wars, I had little list or leisure to write, fearing to be made a history, and shifting daily for my safety." He no longer lived to study, but was forced to study to live.

Sir Edmund Verney, a Royalist like Fuller, expressed the views of many who felt loyal to their King, but were torn by the issues. "I do not like the quarrel, and do heartily wish that the King would yield and consent to what they [Parliament] desire; so that my conscience is concerned only in honour and in gratitude to follow my master. I have eaten his bread, and served him near thirty years, and will not do so base a thing as to forsake him; and choose rather to lose my life (which I am sure to do) to preserve and defend those things which are against my conscience to preserve and defend; for I will deal freely with you, I have no reverence for the bishops, for whom this quarrel [subsists]." England owed much to the fundamental good sense of men like Fuller and Verney.

Bristol during the Civil Wars

The city arms of Bristol

Bristol affords a useful insight into the character of the Civil Wars and the attitudes which lay behind it. Not only was Bristol the second largest city in the kingdom, but it represented a wide cross-range of interests in which the mercantile predominated. Many leading Bristol citizens had lost all patience at Charles's policy. In 1634, for example, Charles I called upon the city to contribute £6,500 ship money, ostensibly to defend English shipping against Turkish and other pirates; but the pretext was a thin veil for a plan to support Catholic Spain against the Protestant Dutch. Many other aspects of personal rule helped to harden Bristol opinion against the King. For example, soap-making was a large Bristol industry, yet Charles I had auctioned off the national soap monopoly to certain London merchants – again, to raise money to support his personal power. West Country merchants felt great anger when told to submit weekly accounts of their soap manufacture to London, as part of these new arrangements.

Charles also sought to discourage Puritan activity in the city. In 1642 he wrote to John Locke, the mayor, complaining of "upstarts in religion." Bristol's answer was couched in strong independent language, and a Royalist force under Sir Ferdinando Gorges was refused admittance through the city gates. However, most of the people of Bristol wanted to be left in peace, to increase their trade and prosperity, and avoid any open clash. When events in London had brought the country to the brink of war in 1642, Bristol refused to support either the King or the Parliamentary leaders. Locke now began preparations for the defence of the city's neutrality against any outside pressure. The three city trained bands were drilled, and the city walls repaired and strengthened, and Bristol Castle properly garrisoned. However, the moderates proved unable to maintain a neutral policy. A group of Puritan residents secretly arranged for a Parliamentary army under Colonel Essex to enter the city. The matter was settled. Nathaniel Fiennes (1608–69) emerged as Bristol's new wartime leader, and when a Royalist plot was discovered, by which an army of 6,000 men commanded by Prince Rupert was to have been let into the city, Fiennes presided over a vengeful bloodletting.

As in London, houses crowded Bristol's bridge

In 1643, however, the tide of war turned against the Puritans. In July, Prince Rupert returned to the West Country with another army, and after a risky engagement managed to occupy parts of the city. After bitter argument with his Puritan colleagues, Fiennes decided to offer a formal surrender to Prince Rupert. Many of his troops now decamped to the Royalist side and began to plunder their own city. Some time later, the unfortunate Fiennes was tried by Parliamentary tribunal under William Prynne, and was sentenced to death; but Oliver Cromwell and Thomas Fairfax intervened to save his life. A lesson that Cromwell learned from the fall of Bristol was the undesirability of leaving towns sympathetic to his cause in amateur hands. From now on, he determined that wherever possible experienced soldiers should be placed in command.

The Custom's house, Bristol

Having been first looted by local deserters and then taxed virtually to ruin for two years by the new Royalist authorities, the people of Bristol must have wondered exactly what or whom they should be supporting. After a major Royalist defeat at Naseby in June, 1645, and the flight of Charles I, Cromwell and Fairfax decided to try and recapture Bristol. When the plans were discovered, Prince Rupert himself returned to take up command of the city garrisons again; at this time Bristol was suffering from a severe epidemic of plague. Early on the morning of 10th September, the Royalist forces were defeated and Prince Rupert sued for terms; Cromwell's New Model Army gave them no quarter, and hundreds of captives were put to death.

In his book, *England's Recovery*, Thomas Sprigg noted the unfortunate plight of the innocent residents and shopkeepers of the city: Bristol looked "more like a prison than a city, and the people more like prisoners than citizens; being brought so low with taxations, so poor in habit, and so dejected in countenance; the streets so noisesome, and the houses so nasty, as that they were unfit to receive friends or freemen till they were cleaned."

Even after Cromwell's authority had been established, Bristol was torn by internal religious strife. After the Royalist priests had been hounded from their churches, the Puritans and Baptists themselves fell

 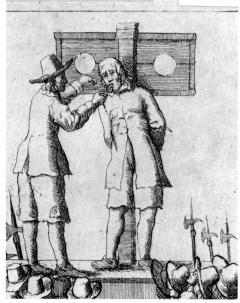

Left James Naylor, reputedly a Quaker, was flogged *centre*, pilloried and
branded *right* for his part in religious unrest in Bristol, 1655

into bitter disputes. The mounting religious frenzy found a focus in the
case of a poor crazed wretch, James Naylor (1616–60), who made a
Christ-like entry into Bristol in 1655. After a long debate, Parliament
condemned him to a vicious public whipping and branding along the
road from Bristol to London. Everyone who had embraced extreme
religious attitudes in their sincere zeal now feared for their lives and
property. London Royalists, Parliamentary freebooters, Papists, Independents, Zealots, informers, corrupt leaders – were the people of
Bristol never to find peace in their time? When one remembers that
similar episodes took place not only in Bristol but throughout the realm
of England for almost twenty years, one need not wonder at the general
joy and sense of relief which followed the Restoration of Charles II, nor
seek too far for the reasons behind apparently sudden and violent
changes of loyalty of men like Samuel Pepys.

Toward the Restoration

After the death of Oliver Cromwell on 3rd September, 1658, Parliament
and the New Model Army seemed quite unable to settle their differ-
ences. There was little sense of direction, and little idea as to what the
method of government should be in the absence of monarchy. Growing
conflicts as to the conduct and financing of the never-ending Civil Wars
undermined the partnership between General John Lambert (1620–94)
and other military leaders with Parliament, and the Restoration of
Charles II was now made virtually certain. In autumn, 1659, anarchy
returned to England when Lambert marched on the House of Commons and formally declared its dissolution. Many leaders now wanted
a return to a politically stable order, which meant one thing: the return
of the King. When Charles II himself met them half-way by promising
"liberty to tender conscience" in his Declaration of Breda (4th April,
1660), his return to England was assured. The following month dele-
gates sailed to Holland bearing their invitation to Charles, and at the
end of the month the son returned to the throne upon which his father
had been executed.

80

4 The Commonwealth of Trade

THE HISTORIAN James Howell approved of the merchant-adventurer. He knew no career "more to be cherished and countenanced with honourable employments than the Merchant-Adventurer." He explained, "For if valiant and dangerous actions do ennoble a Man, and make him merit, surely the Merchant-Adventurer deserves more Honour than any. For he is to encounter not only with Men of all Tempers and Humours (as a French Counsellor hath it), but he contests and tugs oft-time with all the Elements." In Howell's view, the merchant was just as much a gentleman as his country cousins: "Nor do I see how some of our County Squires, who sell Calves and Runts, and their Wives perhaps Cheese and Apples, should be held more genteel than the noble Merchant-Adventurer who sells Silks and Satins, Tissues and Cloths of Gold, Diamonds and Pearl, with Silver and Gold."

Yet during the early Stuart period events did little to stimulate the growth of trade. The monopolies auctioned by the early Stuart kings may have swelled their treasuries, but they kept valuable trades in a few hands. The high customs duties of tonnage and poundage represented heavy burdens for the merchants, and ones they continually grumbled about, especially as the money was used to support the personal power of the monarchy at the expense of Parliament. The merchants also claimed to be inadequately protected against pirate ships; in 1609 it was said that a thousand pirates worked off the Irish coast; and indeed in the period 1609–17, 416 pirate ships were captured.

Cartoon of Alderman Abel with his monopoly of wines, 1641

In the reign of James I, Parliament banned all monopolies, yet Charles I continued to sell a large number of monopolies to those merchants prepared to pay his price. The trades involved were many: alum manufacture at Whitby, brick-making, saltpetre manufacture, tapestry-making, coining of farthings, the manufacture of steel, of guns, of stone pots and jugs, and the smelting of iron ore. One of the most profitable monopolies was tobacco, originally imported by Raleigh in the reign of Queen Elizabeth I: this was made a monopoly for the King. Charles also stopped the new American colony of Virginia from selling tobacco abroad. He made an extra income by setting a duty of four shillings a chaldron on coal exports, and even tried to organize a monopoly on brewing and malting for himself. Merchants too small to

The Mercers' Hall, Cheapside, London

buy these monopolies found themselves cut off from much lucrative business, and protested to Parliament and the King with rising anger as the years passed. Nor were monopolies necessarily efficient: John Pym claimed that the £360,000 annual wine trade monopoly was only worth £30,000 annually to the King. Monopolies were one of the many features of early Stuart rule that helped create a climate of civil war.

The Jacobean period saw a rise in the commercial and maritime power of the Dutch, who were to become England's greatest rivals for European trade. The United Company of Holland competed with the East India Company of England. English and Dutch merchants found themselves in frequent dispute over international fisheries and other commercial rights, and during the later part of the century this rivalry was to help lead to war between the two nations.

Sir Walter Raleigh (1552–1618) wrote in his *Observations on Trade and Commerce* that the Dutch were greater merchants than the English. He attributed this to their low duties, low shipping costs, fast and efficient merchant ships, and their thriving warehouse business: "As regards the storing of merchandize Amsterdam is never without a supply of 700,000 quarters of corn, which they keep always ready besides what they sell; and the like with other commodities, so that if a Dearth of Fish, wine, grain, or anything else begins in the country, forthwith the Dutch are ready with fifty or a hundred ships dispersing themselves at every 'Port-Town' in England trading away their cargoes and carrying of English gold."

Raleigh pointed out that the Dutch had in their hands the greater part of the carrying trade of France, Portugal, Spain, Italy, Turkey, the East Indies, and the West Indies, but argued that London was a much more convenient port "if our merchants would but bend their course for it."

Yet despite these difficulties, and sometimes because of them, English commerce was to find new forms, and new methods of operation, that were to make the seventeenth century an important one in English mercantile growth.

Companies and Capitalists

The foundation of the East India Company in the year 1600 was a symbol of a new age. Companies had, it is true, existed before that date, but the seventeenth century witnessed a new and rapid growth in company activities. Company organization now grew more formal, more enduring.

In its infancy, the East India Company raised fresh capital each time it wished to sponsor a merchant voyage, and months, or even years later, the profits or losses on the voyages would be shared out among the backers when the ship and its crew returned home. This system, however, was felt to involve too much uncertainty, and the East India Company decided to create more continuity by raising its capital for fixed periods, four years at a time. This, in its turn, yielded place to the raising of permanent capital. A new class of speculators sprang up, who made a living from trading in the stock and its intermittent dividends. The jobber also appeared as the middle-man in stock dealings.

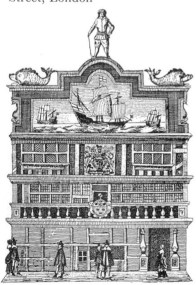

East India House, Leadenhall Street, London

During the seventeenth century new capitalist companies began to compete for supremacy with the old authoritarian guilds which, since medieval times, had dominated traditional crafts and industries. Many guilds complained at these developments, and determined "to strengthen the ramparts of town privileges against the assaults of unrestricted competition."

As the decades passed, the guilds felt growing anxiety about the putting-out system. In this system weaving, for example, ceased to be organized exclusively by master weavers and their journeymen and apprentices. The new employers began to organize their own work forces; a merchant with sufficient capital would "put out" work on commission to cottage-dwellers or others, supplying them with equipment, materials, and tools, and collecting the finished work from them. The system began to flourish, and brought about a natural division of employment. Masterminding the whole process was the employer; his foremen would arrange the delivery and collection of materials from the workmen. When the work was delivered, the employer would sell it in bulk to a city wholesaler, who would in his turn distribute it to local shopkeepers. Sometimes the employer merchanted his own goods, and consolidated an organization involving dozens, even hundreds, of individuals, all of whom owed their livelihood to him. This was to be the new pattern of life for thousands of craftsmen and artisans, until the dawn of the Industrial Revolution two centuries later.

Until the end of the century, England had no bankers in the modern sense of the term, namely a class of men exclusively concerned with raising and applying sources of capital. Banking activities were conducted by businessmen with a wide range of other interests – East India Company magnates, great London or provincial textile merchants, or merchants in gold and other precious commodities. These men also handled foreign currency exchange for the government and other bodies.

In medieval times the lending of money at interest had been condemned by the Church as usury, although merchants had always been able to find practical alternatives – such as claiming fictional falls in exchange rates by the time the loans fell due for repayment. But in the seventeenth century, money-lending threw off these medieval attitudes. An Act of Parliament passed in 1624, which limited interest rates to eight per cent per annum, gave tacit recognition to the new climate.

Credit was becoming an important element in commerce and industry. A textile employer often needed to supply materials to his poorer workers on credit; he might also obtain wool from farmers on credit. Such transactions were often based on written agreements. These "promises to pay" would help the creditor to obtain independent finance for his own business; or they might be discounted by a third party for cash.

The government, too, began to explore new credit facilities, although not on the scale of private merchants. Indeed, without financial credit, the government could not have paid for its part in the Civil Wars. Cromwell's government, indeed, was indebted to £1,500,000. The national debt was to remain a permanent feature of government, and

Silver coin of the East India Company, 1675

The Royal Exchange, where James II was proclaimed king

A sixteenth-century loom

its funding a matter of rising political concern in the eighteenth century.

Yet, despite advances in monetary organization, several more generations were to pass before the Bank of England was founded. This took place in 1694; in this year the new Bank undertook to raise a public loan of £1,200,000 for the government at 8 per cent, and did so in twelve days. In return, it became the first English joint-stock (corporate) bank, although as yet its bills were not legal tender. The real history of English banking belongs to the next century.

The Textile Industry

The textile industry was the most important in England. It was also the oldest. Conducted throughout the kingdom in cottages, farms, and even small manufactories, it was the bulwark of English overseas trade. So important was it, that a proclamation of 1614 prohibited the manufacture of English textiles in foreign staples at Bruges or elsewhere. Henceforth, all English wool had to be spun in England.

Earlier trade restrictions were lifted, which enabled wool-brokers and others to buy wool anywhere in the country, and to sell to clothiers in distant localities. Despite frequent charges of "engrossing" (stockpiling) wool, the overall effect was to produce a freer and more competitive industry. The greatest wool exchange was Bakewell Hall in London.

How did the industry operate in practice? The raw materials were flax imported from Ireland, English wool, and Levantine cotton. Except in parts of the Midlands and the north of England, the old handicraft system of medieval times was giving way to the putting-out system. The farmer would send his wool to the local market, where it was bought by the spinner. When the spinner had spun the wool into yarn, he sold the yarn to the weaver, who sold the finished cloth to a clothier or merchant. The clothier would then sell it in bulk, or make it up into finished goods which were wholesaled to shopkeepers in London and other towns, or were shipped abroad.

The weaver, a contemporary woodcut

Weavers, spinners and dyers used little equipment, generally worth £5 to £20. These craftsmen depended upon a quick turn round of goods, and easily fell under the financial grip of large city merchant clothiers, who would often purchase the equipment for them, and so make them as dependent as if they had been wage-earners. As control of the industry gradually passed from the guilds of weavers, spinners and dyers, the workers themselves were no better off; in many cases they simply found themselves working for new masters. Few could aspire to the riches and power of the successful clothier, with his staff of factors, brokers, clerks, journeymen, and apprentices.

It is thought that the textile industry expanded slightly during the Jacobean period, although the industry was hit by a depression in the 1620s, in which the poorest suffered the most. A Privy Council committee heard a wide range of evidence, and eventually set down many reasons for the slump: the growth of cloth-making abroad was undoubtedly one reason. The drapers complained that England was filled with Dutch and other continental products, whose quality was not adequately checked in public markets. Many English workers complained, too, on the effects of changes of fashion – towards foreign silks, satins, and other stuffs. Nor did the Thirty Years War (1618–48) and other continental hostilities improve English export trade. The merchants voiced many complaints – especially regarding the monopolies purchased from the crown by the big chartered companies. By 1640, London broadcloth exports stood at only a third of the 1606 figure.

Anxious about the effects of the depression, the Privy Council sent out letters to the local justices of the peace. The Council urged them to ensure that craftsmen in their parishes were not cruelly thrown out of work, where they might become a menace to local law and order, and a burden on the community. In an effort to reduce the hardship, measures were taken against those who sought to stockpile wool against better times. A striking measure of the difficult times in the textile industry and elsewhere was that no less than 80,000 Englishmen emigrated to the New World in the period 1620–40.

The Civil Wars in the middle of the century brought another period of hardship for the textile industry. Export shipping was said to be in continual danger, not only from Dutch vessels, but from Royalist privateers roaming coastal waters. Heavy taxation brought about an acute shortage of credit on which the industry had grown to depend; and episodic military action throughout the kingdom hampered communications. Finally, many people felt that English cloth could no longer justify its boast of the best quality in the world, and were not surprised to find that it was losing ground to continental products. Many English craftsmen went to live abroad. Poor quality was, perhaps, the most serious effect of the overthrow of the old guild system, and the slow erosion of the quality control exercised by the guild masters.

By the end of the century, England's greatest industry had undergone a transformation. The various branches of the industry – wool and flax growing, spinning, weaving, dyeing, and finishing – had been forced into more specialization, in order to compete with foreign materials, many of which were now popular among English customers. The textile industry had matured as a commercial enterprise, of which organization, credit, and "employment" had become the main pillars.

Dyeing cloth, early seventeenth century

Other Industries

The most rapid advance in industry was made by coal. After decades of uncontrolled deforestation, timber was becoming a scarce fuel commodity, and more and more people were turning to coal as a domestic fuel. By 1618, it is estimated that two hundred chimney sweeps were employed in London. It is true that England still boasted a few great forests, such as Sherwood Forest and the New Forest, but "deforestation" elsewhere had made the authorities reluctant to allow the wholesale felling of timber. The historian J. U. Nef found that in Elizabeth's time coal was burned "only by the poor who could not afford to buy wood." But early in the reign of James I the situation was becoming worse. Sea coal, brought by coastal vessels from Newcastle to London, multiplied seven times in the period 1580 to 1605.

Most coal was mined from outcrops, and until the later seventeenth

Seal of the coal traders, founded in Newcastle in 1600

Making spectacles in 1659

century the sinking of mine shafts was an exceptional process. The capital expense involved was very great; as indeed was the transportation of coal to distant markets. As a result, in an early stage of its life, the coal industry became dominated by capitalist organization. Miners, unlike other workers, could not work on commission, nor could they afford to buy the tools of their trade. Ironmasters were the largest customers of the coal industry, and consequently grew to be its largest investors; in the seventeenth century the great partnership between iron and coal was forged.

Shipbuilding was another flourishing industry, and Bristol and Newcastle became its chief homes. England's first navy had been created by Henry VIII in the sixteenth century, and the thriving maritime trade which flourished in the wake of sea supremacy demanded more and larger vessels for bringing precious goods, calicoes and silks, dyes, perfumes, spices, and other cargoes from the Orient, and exporting manufactured textiles, metal goods, and other products in return.

The manufacture of salt and glass were two other expanding trades which provided a living to several thousand people, and helped to lay the foundation of England's reputation as an industrial nation.

Freight

England had no railway or canal system in the seventeenth century, and merchants were forced to depend on a poor road system to carry their goods. Good roads were few and far between; the vast majority were unmade dirt tracks, narrow and dangerous. The most familiar figure on the highways was the carrier, who "knew every inch of his road, which might, for miles at a stretch, be a confusion of straggling tracks with never a sign-post, and no light but the glow worm after sundown." (J. Crofts, *Packhorse, Waggon and Post.*)

The carrier had a waggon or pack-horses, which, laden with bales of goods, would wind their way at snail's pace from one destination to another. Often they would carry passengers who were weary of walking, and too poor to travel in style on the stage-coach. A contemporary, Fynes Moryson (1566–1614), felt that "this kind of journeying is so tedious, by reason they must take waggon very early, and comes very late to their Innes, as none but women and people of inferior condition, or strangers . . . use to travel in this sort."

Small carriers found local trade as best they could, moving wherever their custom took them; others preferred to work the same routes. The larger carriers, who might own a dozen or more horses, and employ a staff of carriers, grooms and a clerk, would have a small office in two or three towns, perhaps London, Oxford, Bristol, and Norwich, and advertise their services.

But whichever carrier a tradesman used, the risks were the same. Apart from the weeks and months consumed in the movement of his cargo, there were hazards of snow storms and heavy rains which might obscure the direction of the roads, or block their passage; many a carrier gang became separated and lost. Brigands roamed remote regions, preying on lonely passers-by. The carrier himself might be dishonest. A series of court cases in the seventeenth century clarified the legal responsibility of the carrier toward his cargo. The famous judge, Sir Edward Coke (1549–1634), said that a carrier had certain inherent obligations which he could only escape by a special agreement with his customer. For example, he remained liable for his cargo whatever its value, even when unaware of what he was carrying. For example, a carrier who lost a cargo of tobacco, which hid gold bullion of £100, would be liable for both the bullion and the tobacco.

Few carriers insured their goods. Insurance itself was not yet a very advanced profession, and in any case the risks involved in carriage were too great. It appears that some carriers paid protection money to well-known highwaymen, as a form of insurance. The notorious highwayman William Nevinson, who was eventually hanged in 1684, made regular levies upon carriers using the Great North Road. In deserted regions like this, the villagers' traditional hue-and-cry, or noisy pursuit, was of little avail.

It can easily be imagined how important carriers were in the spreading of news, whether of national or local interest. Indeed, for many small villages and hamlets, the carrier was the only regular means of communication with the outside world; he was postman, government agent, and gossip. In his hands lay the fortunes of many great English merchants and traders.

The Working Classes

The life of every working man and woman in England was intimately affected by the Statute of Apprentices, passed in the reign of Queen Elizabeth I (1563). This famous statute had helped to codify a mass of medieval law and custom relating to working conditions. The Statute dealt with almost every aspect of working life. Shoemakers, bakers, textile workers, brewers, smiths, butchers, and millers were all entitled to a year's security in their trade or craft. Various categories of workers were, however, fated always to remain in the craft in which they had been reared – unmarried people, people aged under thirty, everyone owning property worth less than forty shillings a year, or goods worth less than £10. As a result, the enterprise of a large section of the community was restricted.

A young man could make a good start in life by becoming indentured as an apprentice to a master of his chosen trade. But here, too, obstacles might be set in his path. Apart from a few exceptions in the building industry, a young man could only enter into an apprenticeship if his father owned freehold property worth forty shillings a year. Even then, he would have to face seven years' toil in the house of his master. The working day lasted from dawn until dusk – which made the summer days arduous indeed.

An apprentice might expect rough treatment from an unscrupulous master, a cruel slavedriver more concerned to provide himself with cheap manpower than with training a future craftsman. In theory, an apprentice could seek redress from the local justice of the peace, but everything combined to place him at a social disadvantage.

By a statute passed in the reign of James I, wage levels were supposed to be fixed by the local magistrates. But many magistrates were themselves

London street sellers in the second half of the century, *top* the seller of singing glasses, *centre* the chimney sweep and his boy, *below* ballads for sale

A London apprentice

Fetching water, 1602

masters in a trade, employing their own apprentices, and so had a vested interest in keeping wages to a minimum – even when dealing with cases outside their own trade. The government did make an effort to ensure that wages were kept at a reasonable level, as they were required to do under the Statute of Artificers. In 1614, for example, the justices of Wiltshire summoned all the local clothiers to a meeting to enquire whether any wages had been increased during the last forty years, in proportion to the rising cost of living. But such action does not seem to have been typical.

During the seventeenth century, apprentices became a powerful group, as vocal as many student groups today. For example, during the Civil War in 1643, when it was feared Charles would march on the City of London, the apprentices turned out in force to defend the city gates. Four years later, the London apprentices went on strike, to recover the traditional holidays that the Puritans had abolished: three days at Christmas, Good Friday, Easter Monday, and Whit Monday. At one time, the apprentices were famous for trying to keep London a fit city to live in, for instance by ransacking all the brothels they could find every Shrove Tuesday.

We have a vivid picture of the life of an apprentice, known to us only as "F.K.," who wrote his autobiography under the title *The Unlucky Citizen*. At the age of sixteen, he was apprenticed by his father to a scrivener (clerk or scribe) for eight years. His father had to pay the scrivener a £30 fee, plus a deposit of £100 against the boy's good conduct. The scrivener kept two apprentices, the other being his own son, and although the son was younger than F.K., F.K. was given all the dull work. As well as helping to write legal documents, F.K. wrote: "I was to make clean the Shooes, carry out the Ashes and Dust, sweep the Shop, cleanse the Sink (and a long nasty one it was), draw the Beer, at washing times to fetch up Coals and Kettles . . . then, being grown up to some maturity and understanding, I began to grumble.

"When I have bin seriously a drawing Writings in the Shop and studying and contriving how to order my Covenants the best way, a greasy Kitchen-wench would come and disturb me with one of her Errants, and tell me I must fetch a farthing worth of Mustard, or a pint of Vinegar, or some such mechanical story; nay, my Mistress hath sent me for a Pint of Purl, which when she hath warmed and tasted of, and not liked. I must carry it again to change it."

Three years later at the age of nineteen, he wrote a bitter complaint to his father. "But I was little the better for it," he said. "No sooner was I come into my Master's House, but he seeing me, enters his Closet, from whence fetches a lusty Battoon Cane (the ordinary Weapon with which I was used to be disciplined), and without by your leave, or with your leave, he takes me by the hand, and lifting up his Sword Arm like a Fencer, he gives me a lusty Thwack over the Shoulders (and said) 'Sirrah, I'le teach you to run and make complaints to your Father.'"

F.K. thought that some masters did their very best to drive their own apprentices away. Having engaged perhaps dozens of apprentices, and taken a £50 fee from each, the master so persecuted them that they absconded, and made no effort to recover their money.

It is almost impossible to evaluate the real worth of wages in the seventeenth century. Certainly, they were only measured in shillings and pence. A true assessment would depend upon detailed knowledge of the cost of living, which varied considerably from year to year and from one locality to another. One thing seems to be clear, however. Wages were never expected to support a whole family. A workman was paid only enough to keep himself. His wife, children, and other dependents were all expected to do a full day's work to contribute to the costs of the household.

Above The blacksmith at work. *Right* Country lady spinning outside her home

As industry grew more specialized, the skilled workers became more in demand; the unskilled remained the same. Their wages reflected these trends. Most women in the countryside worked all day in the fields, or sat at home endlessly spinning yarn; children were set to work at any unskilled task that might lie at hand – mending, carrying, sweeping. If the skilled workers drew higher wages than the unskilled, they also seem to have led the more precarious lives. Dependent upon fixed incomes, they always lived at the mercy of fluctuations in the price of bread, yet often had no land of their own from which they could bake a little of their own bread, or keep a cow for milk and butter. It is not surprising that, under these new social pressures, the government should have been forced to pay some attention to the state of the nation's poor.

A contemporary cottage interior

The Poor

The landmark of legislation for the poor in the seventeenth century was the Poor Relief Act of 1601. This statute provided that each parish was to take responsibility for its own poor. The magistrates were ordered to appoint churchwardens or householders to act as overseers, whose task it was to find useful work for paupers. If no work was available, the overseers could impose parish rates to buy raw flax, spinning-wheels and other equipment. The tax would also provide relief to the aged and infirm, and anyone else who could not reasonably be expected to care for himself. Those who were sound in body and who refused work might be sent to the local house of correction, an unpleasant place designed to deter idle vagabonds. At the same time, begging was strictly forbidden.

A beggar and his wife playing on fiddle and bones

Chapel of the leper hospital, Southwark 1636

Where possible, apprenticeships were found for pauper children.

The main drawback of the new system was that it depended upon a tiny local unit – the parish. The overseers were deliberately chosen from the well-to-do classes of the community, and they were naturally reluctant to fix high parish taxes at the expense of their friends and families, especially where the parish poor originally came from other villages. Often, the old or incurably sick were sent on their way, if a pretext could be found, as when their family lived in a near-by parish.

In every way the effective working of the poor law depended upon the goodwill of the justices and other local people. If the statutes were ignored, there was very little that the government could do, without a national system of inspectors or police. During the depression of the 1620s, when the textile industry was at a low ebb, the government took special care to see that the poor law was enforced. This was less out of a sense of altruism than out of a fear that the swollen ranks of the unemployed might provide the nucleus for a popular uprising. At the same time, restrictions were imposed on ale-houses and the brewing of strong beer.

Lack of employment was not the only problem which faced the parishes. In an age of wooden houses, fire risks were very great, and many a family could be ruined by carelessness with an indoor open fire. Outbreaks of plague were another hazard of life. Both calamities added to the problems of administering poor relief.

Apart from official measures, the problem of poverty was dealt with in other ways. Every major town had its almshouses, schools, hospitals, and other charities, endowed by wealthy local families. Many were medieval foundations, others were more recent. Over a period of centuries, these great institutions had come to play a valuable part in English social life, endowed with capital sums large enough to guarantee their future. Many, of course, still survive today in modern forms.

The poor found themselves in a parlous state during the Civil Wars. Their livelihoods destroyed by the national depression, they now faced the indignation of Puritan leaders, to whom work was not merely a necessity of life, but a moral virtue. Paradoxically, the work of charities and of philanthropists was cut back during the Puritan ascendancy, and hardship increased. Puritan preachers were fond of quoting St. Paul: "If any would not work, neither should he eat."

However, Parliament did do something to alleviate hardship. After six successive bad harvests (1646–51) had forced the price of wheat to record levels, steps were taken to ensure that all wheat was sold in the open market, and not hoarded against the future. Improvised poor offices were opened, where the unemployed might meet to seek work. In addition, the price of coal was kept artificially low.

The nation of England might have been slowly growing in wealth and industry during the seventeenth century, yet the lot of those at the lowest levels of society remained a hard and unenviable one. Economic historians have found that the rich were getting richer, the poor poorer. The complex and changing patterns of economic growth were only dimly perceived by contemporaries, who in any case felt less sense of practical duty towards their community than their successors do today.

5 The Restoration

IN 1660, amid almost universal thanksgiving, Charles II was restored to the throne of England. He was to reign until 1685. English people everywhere drank loyal toasts; maypoles were seen again in the villages, and the Puritans were laughed to scorn by the Royalists. But toasts were also drunk to Parliament, which most people now regarded as the monarchy's indissoluble partner. A contemporary wrote that Threadneedle Street was all day long and late at night crowded with people crying out, "A free Parliament! A free Parliament!" so that the air rang again with their noise. When Charles II rode out on horseback, the crowd was so excited that he feared for his personal safety, and to quieten them as he would his children, he said: "Pray be quiet, ye shall have a free Parliament." Charles II was determined not to repeat the fatal errors of his father's reign. Diplomatic compromise would be his policy.

Samuel Pepys left a vivid record in his diary of the general excitement at the Restoration. In Cheapside, he saw a great many bonfires and heard Bow Bells (at St. Mary-le-Bow) and the bells in every other London church joyfully ringing as he walked home. Pepys was overwhelmed by the common joy that was everywhere to be seen. He counted fourteen bonfires between St. Dunstan's and Temple Bar, and at Strand Bridge as many as thirty-one. Every street was filled with the noise and smell of ox-roasts – "the burning of rumps" as these were called in defiance of the old Rump Parliament.

With the Stuarts restored to the throne, scores of men suffered for their part – nearly a generation before – in the trial and execution of Charles I. Thirteen people went to the scaffold even though they had not particularly supported Cromwell in the years between. Major-General John Harrison was one; in fact, he had even been thrown in prison by Cromwell. At his trial in 1661, Harrison proudly stood by what he had done to rid the country of Charles I's despotism. Many ordinary folk must have sympathized, and been saddened by the moment.

"The act of which I stand accused was not a deed performed in a corner. The sound of it has gone forth to most nations, and, in the singular and marvellous conduct of it, has chiefly appeared the sovereign power of Heaven." He added, "I have often, agitated by

Regicides being executed in 1660, *below* beheading, *bottom* hanging

Charles II embarking at Scheveningen, Holland, for his return to England
in 1600

Charles II, a popular woodcut
above and a commemorative
Restoration medal *below*

doubts, offered my addresses, with passionate tears, to the Divine Majesty, and earnestly sought for light and convictions. I still received assurances of a heavenly sanction, and returned from such devout supplications with tranquillity and satisfaction.

"All the allurements of ambition, all the terrors of imprisonment have not been able, during the usurpation of Cromwell, to shake my steady resolution or bend me to a compliance with that deceitful tyrant: and, when invited by him to sit on the right hand of the throne – when offered riches, splendour, and dominion, I have disdainfully rejected all temptations, and neglecting the tears of my friends and family, have still, through every danger, held fast my principles and my integrity."

Harrison refused to say any more after that. He was condemned to death at Charing Cross, and as a traitor, was hung, drawn and quartered. John Evelyn, the diarist, saw the cart carrying away the mangled remains, and cried, "Oh, the miraculous providence of God!"

Like his contemporaries, Evelyn blessed the fact that the Restoration had been achieved without general bloodshed. "It was the Lord's doing," he wrote, declaring that never in the history of the world had there been a like event, "nor so joyful a day and so bright ever seen in this nation."

Under the mask of celebration, processions, and toasts, Restoration England remained in many ways a divided realm. Despite the promises of Charles II, some Parliamentarians doubted whether the idea of the divine right of kings had really been destroyed. Puritans were saddened by the evident change of climate, especially in London, where the playhouses reopened, where drinking and merrymaking returned, where fashions became as flamboyant as they had ever been. Nevertheless, most ordinary folk were glad that the harshness and uncertainty of the Protectorate were ended; a sense of permanence had been restored along with the monarchy. The terrain was familiar once more. The licentiousness of many Royalist supporters was a feature of the period, one most apparent on the London stage. On 8th December,

Cartoon showing a London mob burning the effigy of the Rump
Parliament

1660, Puritans were disgusted to learn that for the first time a woman's
part in a play was to be played by a woman. A verse published in *The
Town* marked the event:

> The woman plays to-day; mistake me not,
> No man in gown, or page in petticoat:
> A woman to my knowledge, yet I can't,
> If I should die, make affidavit on't.
> Do you not twitter, gentlemen? I know
> You will be censuring: do it fairly, though;
> 'Tis possible a virtuous woman may
> Abhor all sorts of looseness, and yet play:
> Play on the stage – where all eyes are upon her.

In the age of the playwrights William Wycherley (1640–1716) and
William Congreve (1670–1729), the playhouse became an arena of
fashion as well as of entertainment. After a visit to the new Drury Lane
playhouse in 1673, Samuel Pepys exclaimed, "Lord! To see the difference of the times and but two years gone!" He noted that the ladies in
the pit were more finely dressed than ever before. Ladies and gentlemen
sometimes wore masks at first nights, rather as playgoers wear evening
dress today; but the fashion declined by the start of Queen Anne's
reign.

Pepys was delighted at improvements made after the Restoration.
The stage, for example, was much lighter; wax candles burned everywhere. The manners of the playgoers had improved since Shakespeare's
time; people showed each other more civility, and the playhouse
became less like the bear (baiting) garden. Pepys noticed, too, that
whereas only two or three fiddlers had provided the music, now Drury
Lane boasted nine or ten. The clean stone floors obviated the need for
dirty rushes everywhere. Even the King and Queen became regular
visitors to Drury Lane.

One of the most popular playwrights of the Restoration period was
William Congreve. He began his career as a barrister, but soon turned

The Red Bull Playhouse, one of
the many opened after 1660

to writing plays, and achieved sudden fame in 1693 with his comedy *The Old Bachelor*. His other plays included *The Double Dealer* (1694), *Love for Love* (1695), and *The Way of the World* (1700). A master of the "comedy of manners," Congreve only once turned his hand to tragedy, *The Mourning Bride* (1697). The Restoration was not an age for tragedy.

Another great playwright of the time was William Wycherley, whose satires have a similar "artificial comedy," evident from their titles – *Love in a Wood* (1671), *The Gentleman Dancing Master* (1672), *The Country Wife* (1673), and *The Plain Dealer* (1674). Although past historians have described Wycherley as licentious or indecent, he is generally regarded as being a master of comedy, as well as a savage satirist.

Coffee-houses and Taverns

The coffee-houses which grew up in London after the Restoration became popular meeting places for gossip, for reading or hiring newspapers, for gambling, and just for quiet relaxation. Yet some people, especially those who hankered after the old Commonwealth days strongly disapproved. One root-and-branch reformer wrote in a pamphlet in 1675: "And for coffee, tea, and chocolate, I know no good they do; only the places where they are sold are convenient for persons to meet in, sit half a day, and discourse with all companies that come in, of state-matters, talking of news, and broaching of lies." Coffee-houses, he claimed, were "very great enemies to diligence and industry, have been the ruin of many serious and hopeful young gentlemen and tradesmen, who, before they frequented these places, were diligent students or shopkeepers, extraordinary husbands of their time as well as money."

The first of the London coffee-houses was opened in 1652, in St. Michael's Alley, Cornhill. The proprietor was a Greek called Pasqua Rose. In his first advertisement he explained that coffee "is an innocent, simple thing, composed into a drink by being dried in an oven and ground to powder, and boiled up with spring water." The coffee had to be drunk "as hot as possibly can be endured, the which will never fetch the skin off the mouth or raise any blisters." He also urged that coffee be drunk for its medicinal qualities: it was supposed to aid digestion, quicken the spirits, and make "the heart lightsome." It was also a remedy for sore eyes, if the face were held over a steaming cup, and for good measure prevented dropsy, gout, defluxion of rheums, headache, spleen, hypochondriac winds, and drowsiness.

The writer of these verses heartily agreed:

> But if you ask, what good does Coffee?
> He'll answer, Sir, don't think I scoff yee,
> If I affirm there's no disease
> Men that have drink it but find ease.
>
> More, it has such reviving power
> 'Twill keep a man awake an houre,
> Nay, make his eyes wide open stare
> Both Sermon time and all the prayer.

Coffee-houses quickly became popular, satisfying a need for a convenient place to meet one's friends, read newspapers, talk business or

William Congreve, one of the most popular of Restoration dramatists

just gossip. By the end of the seventeenth century, London had 3,000 such establishments. A doggerel explained how coffee-houses were known by the signs above their door:

> Which plainly do Spectators tell
> That in that house they *Coffee* sell.
> Some wiser than the rest (no doubt),
> Say they can by the smell find't out;
> In at a door (say they) but thrust
> Your nose, and if you scent *burnt Crust*
> Be sure there's *Coffee* sold that's good,
> For so by most 'tis understood.

People of all classes frequented the coffee-house. These were some of them:

> Here in a corner sits a Phrantick,
> And there stands by a frisking Antick.
> Of all sorts some, and all conditions,
> E'en Vintners, Surgeons, and Physicians.
> The blind, the deaf, the aged cripple
> Do here resort and coffee tipple.

Coffee was not the only drink to be had in such establishments. The London historian, Edward Chamberlayne (1616–1703), wrote that in the free and easy atmosphere of the Restoration a greater variety of drinks were on sale in both taverns and coffee-houses. He lists brandy, coffee, chocolate, tea, aromatick, rum, cider, perry, mead, megethlin, beer, ales, sambidge, betony, scurvy-grass, sage ale, and various others. Some of these drinks were very strong. James Howell sent a bottle of megethlin to a friend on New Year's Day, "the pure juice of the bee, the laborious bee, the king of the insects" – with the warning that not more than one glass should be drunk each morning, and that it should be taken with toast to reduce the "humming of the head."

Coffee-houses often served "snacks" between meals. After Samuel Pepys had taken his wife to see a puppet production of *Bartholomew Fair* in 1661, he took her to the Greyhound Tavern in Fleet Street, "and there drank some rasperry sack and eat some sausages, and so home very merry."

Wine attracted high import duties, but this never discouraged the richest from importing casks for their cellars. "Canary" was an established variety of fortified wine, imported from the Canary Islands, although the historian James Howell considered most of the wine sold under that name in London taverns to be a mixture of rough sherries and malagas. Ale and beer were the standard drinks of the lower classes. However, since English brandy was so cheap, this too was drunk in large quantities. Often it was mixed with the juice of juniper berries, and sold as "geneva" – a forerunner of modern gin. In the next century, the drinking of cheap gin was to become a grave social problem.

Tea was an expensive drink at this time, costing as much as fifty shillings a pound. Only the very rich could afford it, and it was to be a very long time before the English gained their reputation as a nation of tea drinkers. One merchant, Thomas Garray, managed to bring the

Coffee houses became the rage in the gayer, more relaxed years after 1660

price down to around sixteen shillings a pound during the Restoration, but this was still way beyond the pockets of ordinary people. Like the coffee merchants, Garray praised the health-giving qualities of his product. Tea, he claimed, was a truly amazing cure for giddiness, difficult breathing, bad sight, lassitude, hot liver, weak stomach, and overweight.

Sign of the Bell Inn, Knightrider Street, London

Books and Newspapers

Throughout the seventeenth century, books were a very expensive item. In the first place, the manufacturing costs were high. Hand-made rag paper was costly, and the composition of type and binding of books, which both had to be performed by hand, were time-consuming. In any case, the number of people able to read and to afford books was very small. Many books were printed in editions of around a hundred copies, and cost as much then as they do today.

An important innovation took place during the Restoration period, which promoted book sales: this was the subscription. In order to limit the high risks of writing and selling books, the author would prepare a prospectus and circulate it to all those he thought might purchase the book; he could then calculate approximately how many copies to print. It was, in effect, a kind of book club. Indeed, the circulation of these prospectuses became an important factor not only in promoting individual books, but in promoting readership in general. The first really successful subscription was for John Dryden's translation of the works of Virgil, which brought him £1,200 in advance.

Ownership of books was a considerable mark of social distinction. How few private libraries existed at this time is proved by a letter written by John Evelyn to Samuel Pepys in 1689, in which he listed all the ones of which he had knowledge. Nearly all were owned by important churchmen, or by bodies such as the new Society for Promoting Christian Knowledge. Indeed, if Evelyn is correct, the first Englishman to have collected a large private library was the Earl of Anglesey (1614–86). Those who did own books often lavished a great deal of care on them as did the specialist craftsmen of the Broderers' (Embroiderers') Company. In the early part of the century books were sometimes bound in crimson, green, or purple velvet, elaborately embroidered at the edges with silk threads. During the Restoration the richer bindings were more often of red or white satin. Books were sometimes bound in pairs inside the same binding, so that the whole volume had to be turned upside down to read the second book; this practice was common in the case of Bibles and prayer books.

The growth of road communications during the Restoration gave a considerable impetus to the development of a newspaper industry. One of the first important periodicals of this time was the *London Gazette* which was first printed and published from Oxford in 1666. Founded on a French model, the *London Gazette* was devoted almost entirely to government notices and advertisements, and soon became the official government newspaper, as it still is today.

The English commercial and provincial press can really be said to date from the time of Charles II. By the reign of William III (1688–1702), provincial newspapers were flourishing in several places – Norwich, Worcester, Lincoln, Rutland, and Stamford, and soon after in York, Liverpool, Nottingham, Hereford, Bristol, and Exeter. An important feature of the new press was its emphasis upon literary journalism, as distinct from government news and advertisement. The reviewing of new books of all kinds helped disseminate new ideas and give the Restoration its special character of literary activity. Many of these newspapers were circulated in London and provincial coffee-houses.

The first coffee house opened in Fleet Street

John Dryden, prominent member of the literary world

Family Life and Pleasures

Some great families, such as the Russells (ancestors of the Duke of Bedford), divided their time between London and the country – in this case between Bloomsbury and Woburn, forty miles away in Bedfordshire. Moving a great household back and forth needed the planning of a military operation. The goods and chattels of scores of members of the family and their servants and dependents had to be packed and despatched by carrier-waggon, and arrangements had to be made for the care of the deserted house. The Russell family records contain an item of four shillings and sixpence to purchase the laundry soap for "the great wash when the family left London." Dozens of washerwomen and cleaners had to be hired at a shilling or one shilling and sixpence a day to "scour and wash the rooms," under the supervision of a housekeeper. One advantage of living in both town and country was that fresh food was always to be had from the family estate, including delicacies such as oranges, peaches, and asparagus (although asparagus was also to be had from market gardens in Battersea).

Those of less affluent circumstances, who lived permanently in London, relied upon the new metropolitan markets – Covent Garden, Spitalfields (chartered by Charles II in 1680), and Clare Market, established in 1657. In addition, Londoners were served by the older markets which had their origins in medieval times – Billingsgate (fish), Leadenhall (poultry), and Smithfield (meat). Villages on London's outskirts were often known for a special produce – we have already mentioned the asparagus of Battersea. Hackney was known for its butter and Stratford-le-Bow for its bread, freshly baked and stamped with a seal.

Meals were eaten with more attention to manners than in the Jacobean period. This is not to say that public rowdiness was not sometimes recorded. Sir John Reresby, Governor of York, quarrelled with a fellow guest at a dinner in 1660, and wrote in his *Memoirs*, "We should have fought the next day, but considering the better of it, he submitted – though it was he who received the affront, for I threw a glass of wine in his face." Loyal toasts were a great part of dinners in the Restoration period, and men always removed their hats for such occasions. Toasts were taken very seriously – each time the glass or tankard had to be drained to the last dregs, and often the host would propose a toast to all his guests in turn.

As we have already seen, a number of new drinks were becoming popular at this time. Food was splendidly served in great communal dishes, and considerable ingenuity was shown in its preparation and display. Salads were a very popular dish, and their ingredients often included such exotic elements as rosemary, borage, violets, rue, broom buds, and cowslips, dressed, as John Evelyn recommended, with "some acetous juice . . . to give them a grateful gust and vehicle."

The lady of the house continued to lead a crowded and varied life. Much of her recreation took the form of handicrafts, and in this respect her existence did not differ greatly from that of her mother and grandmother.

The most popular handicraft was fine needlework. Many women of the time were highly skilled at sewing and embroidery, which were part of the essential education of young girls, designed to help them improve and decorate their homes. Shirts, dresses, and other garments were elaborately embroidered, and beautifully detailed covers with beads and threads were worked for cabinets, boxes, and devotional books. Tapestries and samplers were made as wall hangings and gave houses a rather more cheerful aspect than they enjoyed in the Jacobean years. Sometimes, women used designs taught to them by their mothers, at others they worked from the pattern books which had been popular from Queen Elizabeth's reign. Two of the best-selling pattern books were *The Needles Excellency* (1640) by John Taylor, and Richard Shorleyker's *Schole House of the Needle* (1632).

Jacobean England, as we have seen, had been an age of formalism in dress and manners. This formalism had dominated everyone's lives during the Cromwellian regime, and the reaction after 1660 was all the greater. Some families, it is true, sought to preserve the old traditions, but most of them who could afford it began to embrace high fashion and extravagant manners. The most authentic picture of middle-class life and pleasures of this period is, of course, to be found in Samuel Pepys' own *Diary*. Others have preferred to satirize it. Sir George Savile, first Marquis of Halifax (1630–95), has left posterity a damning sketch of the empty lives of the great, in his famous *Advice to his Daughter*: "She eats her breakfast half-an-hour before dinner, to be at greater liberty to afflict the company her acquaintance, who are already cloyed with her . . . she setteth out like a ship out of the harbour, laden with trifles . . . at her return she repeateth to her faithful waiting woman the triumphs of that day's impertinence; then, wrapped up in flattery and clean linen, goeth to bed so satisfied." It was not an attractive advertisement.

The Restoration saw great changes in fashion. The drab grey colours of Puritan days were giving way to gaiety and extravagance. Samuel Pepys remembered seeing the King and Queen riding in Hyde Park in 1663. The Queen was wearing a white-laced waistcoat and a crimson short petticoat, with her hair dressed "*à la negligence*, mighty pretty." Pepys followed the party to Whitehall Palace, where he observed the ladies "fiddling with their hats and feathers, and changing and trying one another's by another's head, and laughing."

London parks and gardens were thronged with families, servants, and children taking the air together. One famous strolling-place was Spring Garden near Charing Cross, described by a contemporary in *A Character of England*:

"The inclosure is not disagreeable, for the solemnness of the grove, the warbling of the birds, and as it opens into the spacious walks of St. James's. But the company walk in it at such a rate as you would think all the ladies were so many Atalantas contending with their wooers . . . the thickets of the garden seem to be contrived to all advantages of gallantry, after they have been refreshed with the collation, which is here seldom omitted, at a certain cabaret in the middle of this paradise, where the forbidden fruits are certain trifling tarts, neats-tongues, salacious meats, and bad Rhenish wine."

Now that the shadow of the Puritan Protectorate had been lifted, people were free to enjoy themselves again, whether on Sunday or on any other day of the week. A new ebullience appears in descriptions of English life at this time. The seventeenth-century historian, Edward Chamberlayne, gave a catalogue of pleasures in his *Present State of England*. He wrote:

"For variety of Divertisements, Sports and Recreations, no Nation doth excel the English. The King hath abroad his Forests, Chases, and Parks, full of variety of Game; for Hunting Red and Fallow Deer, Foxes, Otters, Hawking, his Paddock-Courses, Horse-Races, *etc.*, and at home, Tennis, Pelmel, Billiard, Comedies, Opera, Mascarades, Balls, Ballets, *etc.* The Nobility and Gentry have their Parks, Warrens, Decoys, Paddock-Courses, Horse-Races, Hunting, Coursing, Fishing, Fowling, Hawking, Setting-Dogs, Tumblers, Lurchers, Duck-hunting, Cock-fighting, Guns for Birding, Low-Bells, Bat-Fowling, Angling, Nets, Tennis, Bowling, Billiards, Tables, Chess, Draughts, Cards, Dice,

The Market Cross, Winchester

99

Country pursuits, *left* angling and *right* for the rich, hunting pheasants with hawks

Catches, Questions, Purposes, Stage-Plays, Masks, Balls, Dancing, Singing, all sorts of Musical Instruments, *etc.* The citizen and peasants have Hand-Ball, Foot-Ball, Skittles, or Nine Pins, Shovel-Board, Stow-Ball, Coffe, Trol Madams, Cudgels, Bear-baiting, Bull-baiting, Shuttlecock, Bowling, Quoits, Leaping, Wrestling, Pitching the Bar, and Ringing of Bells, a Recreation used in no other Country of the World.''

Every sport had its supporters and detractors. Every foreigner who came to England, said Chamberlayne, condemned cock-fighting as too childish and unsuitable an occupation for the gentry; this was a sport for the common people. The common people themselves apparently disapproved of bull-baiting and bear-baiting as too cruel, and those with a pride in civic affairs opposed football and "throwing at cocks" as "very uncivil and barbarous within the city."

Fencing was popular among gentlemen, and afforded amusement to spectators. Josevin de Rochefort, whose travels in England were published in 1672, wrote that fencing masters frequently provoked duels, in order to show off their undoubted skills. Often they would parade through the town with drums and trumpets to inform the local inhabitants of the great occasion. Rochefort remembered one such duel, performed on a public stage, where the agile fencing masters stripped to their waists, "skirmishing a long time without any wounds." But after a few minutes the duel began in earnest, with the emphasis upon the cut rather than the "French push." One of the combatants almost had his wrist severed, but after it had been heavily dressed and he had fortified himself with wine, he returned to the stage and avenged himself by slicing off his opponent's ear. The fight still continued, but Rochefort noticed that the two fencing masters took good care not to do each other any more unnecessary damage. In the end the taller of the two won the duel, and both duellists left the stage to the cheers of the onlookers. "For my part," concluded Rochefort, "I should have had more pleasure in seeing the battle of the bears and dogs which was fought the following day." But with the return of the Royalist regime, fencing was to remain a gentleman's usual remedy for a slight on his honour.

Card games returned to popularity with the Restoration, as the poet Charles Cotton (1630–87) wrote in *The Compleat Gamester* (1674).

Left A lady's dressing-room in the seventeenth century. *Right* Enjoying the chase, 1685

Cotton listed twelve games, of which *primero* was one of the oldest and most popular. A similar game was *ombre*; others included whist, so named "from the silence that is to be observed in the play," slam, bassett (a round game with a banker), lanterloo, beast, bragg, banka-falet, cribbage, gleek, and boneace. Cotton implies that cheating was a common pastime: "If you mark your cards aforehand, so as to know them by the back side, you know how to make your advantage." Most card games seem to have been played for money, as were games of dice.

More innocent were the family theatricals staged at home. John Stewkeley remarked that "this is a much cheaper way to have their company severally." In an age of loosening moral standards, Stewkeley took care to censor his own entertainments: "I did take out of the play what I thought a little modest and impertinent, and the spectators had almost put them out with commending them so loud, as they were acting." Without the modern conveniences of radio and television, families of the seventeenth century had to use their own resources, and usually did so with much enjoyment and ingenuity.

Popular games of the day, *above* billiards, *below* boys' sports, and *bottom* tennis

Music and dancing were popular, too, and the greater houses employed their own resident pipers and fiddlers. The less wealthy might sometimes hire a small ensemble to provide entertainment for a wedding, birthday, or other special occasion. Pepys enjoyed singing, as his diary indicates. After a picnic by the Thames in May, 1669, he remembered "my wife and I singing, to my great content." It was part of the education of sons and daughters of good homes to learn one or more musical instruments, for example the lute, viol, guitar, and the violin which first became popular during the latter part of the century. Keyboard instruments included the virginal and spinet, which had been played for many generations, and the harpsichord, which Pepys and John Evelyn both heard for the first time in 1664. In Evelyn's ears, it sounded like a very modern and highly mechanized contraption, "with gut-strings, sounding like a concert of viols with an organ, made vocal by a wheel, and a zone of parchment that rubbed horizontally against the strings."

Other popular instruments of the time included the dulcimer, harp, flute, flageolet, trumpet, recorder, horn, and – especially in the villages

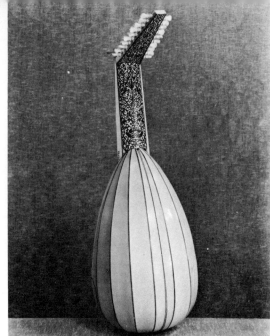

Music played an important part in Restoration society, *left* an octave spinet, *right* a lute

Above Fencing with rapiers, 1667

Below Heraldic playing cards, 1678

– handbells. *The School of Recreation* (1684) approved handbells, for their "mathematical invention delighting the mind," as well as for "the violence of its exercise bringing health to the body, causing it to transpire plentifully, and by sweats dissipate and expel those fulginous thick vapours which idleness, effeminacy, and delicacy subject men to." Almost every seventeenth-century pleasure seemed to require elaborate moral justification.

The great annual festivals of the Church all brought games and entertainments with them, and were looked forward to for that reason. At Eastertime, many English villages became the scene of egg-rolling races. At Whitsun, parishes held church-ales to raise money for church-building and decoration. The biographer John Aubrey (1626–97) wrote, "The housekeepers met and were merry and gave their charity." In some localities the villagers elected a garlanded Lord and Lady to preside over the festivities and lead processions along the lanes. These festivals always attracted great crowds, and professional entertainers such as street musicians, jugglers, and mummers and bull and bear baiters. A great deal of strong local ale was drunk, and parish records often contain references to fist fights, damage to property, and other disturbances. One of the greatest annual festivals was the Eve of May. Now that the Puritan regime had been ended, maypoles were erected once more on village greens, and may-dancing and morris-dancing were enthusiastically revived; few people understood their pagan origins.

During the Protectorate, the Church's greatest festival – Christmas – had been declared an ordinary working day (unless it happened to fall on the Sabbath). Everyone who had continued to hold Christmas celebrations in defiance of the laws was fined or whipped. Even Lord Fairfax was fined five shillings in 1655 for illegally attending "a comedy or stage play at Gillinge at Christmas last." But after the Restoration, Christmas too returned to its place in the calendar as the greatest festival of the year.

6 Plague and Fire

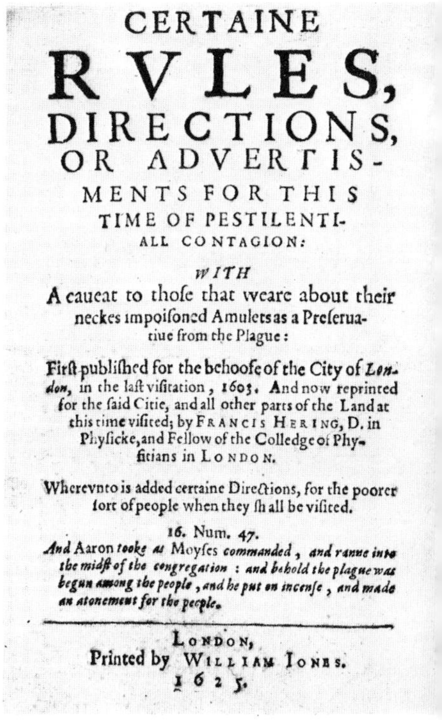

LIKE MANY other Londoners, John Evelyn complained bitterly about the polluted atmosphere. In *Fumigium* (1661) he wrote, "It is this smoke which obscures our churches and makes our palaces look old, which fouls our clothes and corrupts the waters. . . . It is this which scatters and strews about those black and smutty atoms upon all things where it comes, insinuating itself into our very secret cabinets and most precious repositories."

The reason for the foul air was, according to Evelyn, the use of impure Newcastle coal for fuel. If contemporaries are to be believed, London was almost perpetually wreathed and shrouded in fog.

Despite continual protests, little was done to improve public health. As we have seen earlier in these pages, the Thames and Fleet rivers were open sewers; and the houses of London were cramped together often with little light or air. In these conditions, disease could spread quickly and easily; no one could feel safe from such a virulent infection as the bubonic plague which had visited England at intervals throughout her history. In the reign of Elizabeth I, in 1569, the sale of fruit in the streets had been forbidden, because of the risk of plague. In 1635 over half the people of Newcastle perished from a sudden epidemic of bubonic plague. In 1665 cherries, gooseberries, and melons were among the fruits thought to carry the plague. Just four years before the outbreak of the Great Plague in London, Samuel Pepys had anxiously written in his *Diary*: "In the afternoon had notice that my Lord Hinchinbrooke is fallen ill, which I fear is with the fruit that I did give them on Saturday last at my house; so in the evening I went thither and there found him very ill, and in great fear of the smallpox."

Curiously, several people prophesied the Great Plague. The Reverend Thomas Reeve foretold the coming of plague in a pamphlet of 1657. He saw it as a punishment for the nation's sins. "What inventions shall ye then be put to . . . when your sins shall have shut up all the conduits of the city, when ye shall see no men of your incorporation, but the mangled citizen; nor hear no noise in your streets but the crys, the shrieks, the yells and pangs of gasping, dying men; when among the throngs of associates not a man will own you or come near you?"

And, remarkably enough, he also later preached a sermon foretelling the great fire: "Can sin and the City's safety, can impenitence and

CERTAINE
RVLES,
DIRECTIONS,
OR ADVERTIS-
MENTS FOR THIS
TIME OF PESTILENTI-
ALL CONTAGION:

WITH
A caueat to thofe that weare about their neckes impoifoned Amulets as a Preferuatiue from the Plague:

Firft publifhed for the behoofe of the City of London, in the laft vifitation, 1603. And now reprinted for the faid Citie, and all other parts of the Land at this time vifited; by FRANCIS HERING, D. in Phyficke, and Fellow of the Colledge of Phyfitians in LONDON.

Wherevnto is added certaine Directions, for the poorer fort of people when they fhall be vifited.

16. Num. 47.
And Aaron tooke as Moyfes commanded, and ranne into the midft of the congregation : and behold the plague was begun among the people, and he put on incenfe, and made an atonement for the people.

LONDON,
Printed by WILLIAM IONES.
1625.

Titlepage of one of the many pamphlets of instructions and remedies for outbreaks of plague

Daniel Defoe, the author

impurity stand long together? Fear you not some plague, some coal blown with the breath of the Almighty, that may sparkle and kindle, and burn you to such cinders that not a wall or pillar may be left to testify the remembrance of the City?"

Daniel Defoe (1660–1731), aged five when the plague struck London, later wrote a graphic account of his experiences, remembering how people had seen comets in the sky, a portent of disaster: "In the first place, a blazing star or comet appeared for several months before the plague, as there did the year after another, a little before the fire. The old women and the phlegmatic hypochondriac part of the other sex, whom I could almost call old women too, remarked (especially afterward, though not till both those judgments were over) that those two comets passed directly over the city, and that so very near the houses

Citizens fleeing from London during an outbreak of plague in 1630

A
JOURNAL
OF THE
Plague Year:
BEING
Obfervations or Memorials,
Of the moft Remarkable
OCCURRENCES,
As well
PUBLICK as PRIVATE,
Which happened in
LONDON
During the laft
GREAT VISITATION
In 1665.

Written by a CITIZEN who continued all the
while in London. Never made publick before

LONDON:

that it was plain they imparted something peculiar to the city alone; that the comet before the pestilence was of a faint, dull, languid colour, and its motion very heavy, solemn and slow; but that the comet before the fire was bright and sparkling, or, as others said, flaming, and its motion swift and furious; and that accordingly one foretold a heavy judgment slow but severe, terrible and frightful, as was the plague.

"But the other foretold a stroke, sudden, swift and fiery as the conflagration. Nay, so particular some people were, that as they looked upon that comet preceding the fire, they fancied that they not only saw it pass swiftly and fiercely, and could perceive the motion with their eye, but even they heard it; that it made a rushing, mighty noise, fierce and terrible, though at a distance, and but just perceivable."

The last serious outbreak of plague had occurred in the year 1630, when many Londoners were forced to flee their homes and seek the sanctuary of the surrounding countryside. The first signs of the great plague were seen in 1663, when it was raging in Amsterdam across the English Channel; Dutch ships were placed in quarantine. Despite strenuous efforts by the authorities, the plague did at last find its way into England. The first recorded death took place in London in December, 1664, and several more occurred during the following spring.

When the plague first appeared in London in 1665, most people ignored it. Sir Ralph Verney joked, "'Tis plaguey news that the plague has come to Southwark!" But very quickly panic spread, and people realized the outbreak was a serious one.

On 30th April, 1665, Samuel Pepys wrote fearfully in his *Diary*, "Great fears of the sicknesse here in the City, it being said that two or three houses are already shut up. God preserve us all!" Men in the City like Sir Ralph Verney feared that the plague would ruin investment: "'Tis an ill time to put out money for the feare of the Plague makes many willing to take their Estates out of the Goldsmiths' hands, and the King's greate want of money makes many very unwilling to lend any money to these that advance great summs for him."

The rat-catcher and his cat, few people realised that rats spread the disease

In June everyone who could left London – on foot, in coaches, carriages, or carts. A stampede developed, stopped only by villagers outside London, armed with pitchforks to keep the infection at bay. Then, as Sir Walter Besant wrote, "The mortality rising daily by leaps and bounds, the people sat down in their houses to die, or wandered disconsolately about the streets, marking the crosses on the doors with sinking hearts." Yet some people stayed – the Lord Mayor, the Sheriffs, the Aldermen, the Archbishop of Canterbury, the Duke of Albemarle, and others. But the Court left, and the judges moved to the safety of Oxford. The physicians left, saying they had to go with their patients – as did most priests, saying they had to go with their flock. Thousands were left in London to die.

The City of Death

Shops were shut down, business ceased, ships lay unladen in the port of London, no one had any wages, there were no street cries, no church bells, few children. Nonconformist preachers took their chance to seize the churches, crying that the kingdom of God was at hand; quack doctors sold useless cures. People thrown out of work found jobs as gravediggers, searchers, and undertakers. Infected houses soon had foot-long red crosses on their doors. Bartholomew Fair was banned. Pepys wrote in September, 1665, "What a sad time it is, to see no boats upon the river, and grass grows all up and down Whitehall Court, and nobody but wretches in the street!"

The Reverend Thomas Vincent wrote a tract, called *God's Terrible Voice to the City* in which he gave an eyewitness account: "In August how dreadful is the increase! Now the cloud is very black, and the storm comes down upon us very sharp. Now death rides triumphantly on his pale horse through our streets, and breaks into every house where any inhabitants are to be found." In Vincent's words, people were falling as thick as leaves in autumn; a dismal solitude reigned in London streets; every day looked like the Sabbath, observed more solemnly than ever before. Shops were shuttered, bolted and barred, people rarely seen walking about. The grass began to spring up in some places; a deep silence fell in every street, especially within the city walls. "No prancing horses, no rattling coaches, no calling on customers nor

Corpse bearers were in constant danger of disease

Fires were lit to try and purify the air of the London streets, and once a
house had the dreaded cross on it few would go into it

offering wares, no London cries sounding in the ears." The only sounds
were the groans of dying persons breathing their last breath, and the
funeral knells of those about to be hauled to their graves.

Most of the houses were now plague-ridden, and no longer bothered
to put up their shutters. The well mingled amongst the sick, who would
otherwise have been left to their fate. Now, in some places, where the
people stayed behind, not one house in a hundred remained free of
infection, and in many houses half the family perished. Vincent
mourned at how many parents had to carry their children with them
to the grave. In the middle of the summer, 1665, the nights grew too
short to bury the dead; the whole day was hardly long enough for the
task. Not even £1,000 a week given by the King, or £600 a week given
by the City, could feed those that remained, and starvation increased
the death toll. All the while, the sun of that extremely hot summer beat
down; no rain fell to wash the streets or purify the air.

Vincent, who remained in the capital throughout the terror, described the red crosses which people daubed on their doors as a sign of
plague: "It was very Dismal to behold the Red Crosses, and read in
great letters *Lord Have Mercy Upon Us* on the doors, and Watchmen
standing beside them with Halberts, and such a solitude about those
places, and people passing by them so gingerly and with such fearful
looks, as if they had been lined with enemies in ambush that waited to
destroy them."

Old women were employed as "searchers of the dead." They
reported each day to the parish clerks, and the rising weekly death
figures were then published in the *Bills of Mortality*.

Superstitious people clutched at cheap charms and spells to protect

Titlepage of a *Bill of Mortality*,
the official record of deaths in
1665

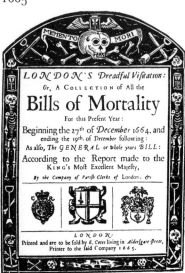

Solomon Eagle, one of the religious fanatics who appeared at the time claiming that the Plague was God's punishment for evil ways

themselves, and many of them bought engraved medallions from pedlars with the legend ABRACADABRA. Others bought little tokens with the Jesuits' mark in a cross.

In mid-1665, however, the plague seemed to be on the decline, and the people rushed to church to give thanks. King Charles and his Court prepared to return from Oxford to London. Clarendon attributed the passing of the danger to a severe early frost: "The weather was as it could be wished, deep snow and terrible frost, which very probably stopped the spreading of the infection, though it might put an end to those who were already infected, as it did, for in a week or two the number of the dead was very little diminished."

No one knew exactly what the casualties were. Newspapers like L'Estrange's *Intelligencer* deliberately published low figures to try and allay fears, and even the *Bills of Mortality* could not be relied on. Clarendon explained that the frequent deaths of the clerks and sextons of parishes hindered the exact account every week; also the vast numbers buried in the fields were never counted. Few of the Anabaptists and other extreme religious sects in the city left their homes; perhaps they did not fear the judgment of God. Many of them died, and no churchwarden or other officer recorded the fact. Burials were found in kitchen gardens or near-by open fields.

But hopes for the decline of the plague in mid-1665 proved ill-founded. On 7th June, Pepys had seen for himself the first ominous red crosses on house doors: "This day, much against my will, I did in Drury Lane see two or three houses marked with a red cross upon the doors, and *Lord Have Mercy Upon Us* writ there; which was a sad sight to me, being the first of the kind that, to my remembrance, I ever saw.

Watchmen guarded infected houses to stop people escaping

It put me into an ill conception of myself and my smell, so that I was forced to buy some roll-tobacco to smell to and chew, which took away the apprehension." As the dreadful truth dawned on everyone – that this might be the worst outbreak since the Black Death – the wholesale evacuation of London began in earnest. Pepys wrote on 21st June: "To the Cross Keys at Cripplegate, where I find all the towne almost going out of towne, the coaches and waggons being all full of people going into the country." The very next day, Pepys decided to send his mother into the safety of the countryside.

In later years, Defoe recalled how the Thames had been filled with small boats of families escaping with as much as they could carry. The watermen on the river above London Bridge ferried them up the river as far as they could go. Many of them had whole families in their boats,

Left Corpses being hurriedly buried and *right* plague carts for carrying corpses and coffins, 1665

covered with tilts and bales, and taking straw for their lodging. The refugees laid the straw along the shore in the marshes, some of them putting up little tents with boat sails, and there they sheltered during the day; at night they slept inside the boats. The river banks were lined with refugee families living as best they could.

At the height of the plague people began to fear the Judgment of God. Vincent declaimed: "The old drunkards, and swearers, and unclean persons, see many fellow-sinners fall before their faces, expecting every hour themselves to be smitten; and the very sinking fears they have of the Plague, hath brought the Plague and Death upon many; some by the sight of a Coffin in the Streets, have fallen into a shivering, and immediately the Disease hath assaulted them, and Serjeant Death hath arrested them."

A Puritan minister, Richard Baxter (1615–91), however, took a more realistic view. He explained that as the rich people deserted the city the greatest blow fell on the poor. At the first, few of the more pious people died, and these then began to be "puffed up and boast of the great difference which God did make." But soon after, they began to die like everyone else.

No precaution was too great. Defoe recalled the care people had taken whilst shopping for food. When buying a joint of meat in the

Samuel Pepys the diarist

market, customers would not take it from the butcher's hand, but lifted it off the hooks themselves. Equally, the butcher would not touch the money; he kept the money in a pot full of vinegar, which he used specially for that purpose. The buyer always carried plenty of small change to make up any odd sum, so that he did not have to take coins from the butcher. They carried bottles of scent and perfume with them and every other means that could be used. But since the poor could not even do these things, they suffered more than the rest.

As the plague cast its shadow over all London with the advent of the warm weather, the shops became deserted. No one was at work, no one earned any wages, trade stopped.

Those who were left behind in London had to make do as best they could. A major problem was the lack of water; even those families who

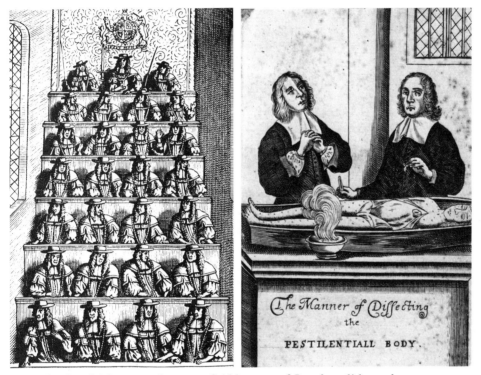

The Lord Mayor and court of Aldermen of London did much to stop panic during the plague and issued health certificates to people leaving London. *Right* Dissecting a victim of the Plague

had a member well enough to fetch it could not easily find water pure enough to drink. Many people died from malnutrition, and want of care, and the will to live was sapped by the sight of parents, children, friends, and acquaintances being taken each day to the mass graves.

According to physicians who kept records, the symptoms of the bubonic plague were frightful. The first signs were feverish sweating, followed soon after by the appearance of dark red blotches on the skin, all over the body. As the plague spread through the body, these erupted into large swellings sometimes several inches across, which eventually burst. One physician, Nathaniel Hodges (1630–84), has left a detailed account of his experiences during these grim months. He made it a rule never to stay in a plague-ridden household too long, and to leave the

One of the many quack doctors who sold infallible "cures"

moment he began to feel himself sweating. On returning home, he would rest, and drink strong liquor to combat the infection.

In such a crisis, people would clutch at any straw which seemed to offer the hope of cure. One pamphlet published during 1665 recommended that live pigeons be used to suck the venom from the sores. Even the august College of Physicians could prescribe no better remedy than onions: "Take a great onion, hollow it, put it into a fig, rue out small, and a dram of Venice treacle . . . apply it hot to the tumour." One Dr. Boghurst wrote that remedies like this: "put them to as much paine as if they had been on the rack, worse than Deathe itself!"

The City of London took what action it could. Every householder was ordered to clean the street in front of his door; orders were made to regulate burials, for instance requiring all graves to be at least six feet deep, preventing children from attending funerals, and banning the lying-in of corpses in churches or homes. But the infection was too widespread for these measures to achieve much. Vincent wailed, "Now the grave doth open its mouth without measure." Mass graves soon had to be dug, as Defoe recalled: "Into these pits they had put perhaps fifty or sixty bodies each; then they made larger holes, wherein they buried all that the cart brought in a week, which, by the middle to the end of August, came to from 200 to 400 a week; and they could not well dig them larger, because of the order of the magistrates confining them to leave no bodies within six feet of the surface; and the water coming on at about seventeen or eighteen feet, they could not well, I say, put more in one pit." At nights, men brought carts round the silent streets, crying, "Bring out your dead!"

Defoe heard tell of a drunken street musician who was "carted away" by mistake: "As soon as the cart stopped the fellow awaked and struggled a little to get his head out from among the dead bodies, when, raising himself up in the cart he called out, 'Hey, where am I?' This frighted the fellow that attended about the work; but after some pause John Hayward, recovering himself, said, 'Lord bless us. There's somebody in the cart not quite dead!' So another called to him and said, 'Who are you?' The fellow answered, 'I am the poor piper. Where am I?' 'Where are you?' says Hayward. 'Why, you are in the dead-cart, and we are going to bury you.' 'But I ain't dead though, am I?' says the piper, which made them laugh a little, though, as John said, they were heartily frighted at first: so they helped the poor fellow down and he went about his business."

Early in September, huge bonfires were lit in an effort to burn the infection in the air but they did not seem to have much effect except to use up tons of precious coal every week. During November, 1665, however, the plague at last showed signs of abating, although many people refused to believe it. Pepys, like everyone else, was going about asking how many of his friends and acquaintances were still alive. Clarendon noted that the greatest number of the dead consisted of women and children, and the lowest and poorest sort of people; apparently few of the "wealthy or quality" died.

Gradually, people made their way back into the city of death. The King and Court returned soon after Christmas. Pepys wrote: "Lord!

what staring to see a nobleman's coach come to town. And porters everywhere bow to us, and such begging of beggars! And a delightful thing is to see the towne full of people again as now it is; and shops begin to open."

Daniel Defoe wrote that the doctors and clergymen who had deserted London in her time of need were bitterly reproached by the people. They were called deserters, and bills were posted on their doors, reading, "Here is a doctor to be let!" Many physicians moved away from their homes to start a new career elsewhere. The same was true of the clergy, towards whom the people were very abusive, writing verses on the church-door such as: "Here is a pulpit to be let!" or "To be sold!"

The death toll was enormous. According to the Nonconformist minister Richard Baxter, deaths in London alone had exceeded 100,000 in 1665; and one Dr. Gumble, who saw all the official reports, calculated that as many again had died outside London, as the evacuees had carried out the infection with them. Half a generation of children had been wiped out. It had been the worst holocaust to strike England in three centuries.

Start of the Great Fire

During previous generations, London had suffered repeatedly from fire damage. In a fire of 1637 part of London Bridge had been destroyed. St. Paul's Cathedral itself had been ravaged several times before. London had no effective fire-fighting force, and depended upon the goodwill and organization of local residents for effective action. James Howell had written in *Londinopolis* (1657) that "There's no place . . . better armed against the fury of the fire; for besides the pitched buckets that hang in the Churches and Halls, there are divers new engines for that purpose." By engines he meant small hand-operated watersquirts. The only other tools were buckets of water and firehooks, used to pull down walls in order to contain the blaze.

A further difficulty of fire-fighting in seventeenth-century London was the property rights bitterly defended by every small householder and trader. The authorities often feared to destroy their buildings to prevent the fire, unwilling to risk the high compensation payments which would be claimed. Such a situation was fraught with danger.

Isaac Ragg, bellman or night-watchman in Holborn, London

After the holocaust of 1665, few people could have imagined what fate was in store for the City of London in the following year. The fire began in the dead of night. At about 3 a.m. on Sunday morning, 2nd September, 1666, a small fire broke out in Farryner's bakery in the narrow Pudding Lane in the City of London. This house, like all the others in the lane, was made of wood and pitch; the lane was so narrow, and the houses overhung so far that the buildings almost touched each other at the top. The fire quickly spread, and set ablaze the Star Inn, whose courtyard was piled high with hay and straw. No one had time to do anything but get out as fast as possible. Hundreds of tons of inflammable goods lay in the warehouses in nearby Thames Street – butter, cheese, wine, oil, sugar, hemp, flax, tar, pitch, resin, brimstone, rope, hops, timber, and coal. The water machines of London Bridge

London before devastation by the Great Fire, a scale model

were burned with the bridge; the blaze soon became so fierce that the pitiful water engines of the time could not get near it.

Samuel Pepys described the early hours of the fire in his diary. He went down to the waterside, and there got a boat and passed under London Bridge, and there saw "a lamentable fire." Even while he watched, the fire was racing through the streets. Everybody struggled to save their goods by flinging them into the river or bringing them into lighters moored close by. Poor people stayed in their houses until the last possible moment of escape and then ran into boats, or clambered along the waterfront from one pair of stairs to another. London's best-known residents, the pigeons, hovered about the windows and balconies until they burned their wings and fell down. Having watched the fire for an hour, and seeing no one to quench it, "but only to remove their goods, and leave all to the fire," Pepys went down to Whitehall to make one of the first reports to the King. "So I was called for, and did tell the King and Duke of York what I saw, and that unless His Majesty did command houses to be pulled down, nothing could stop the fire."

A little while after, Pepys met the Lord Mayor in Canning Street. The Lord Mayor was "like a man spent." He was crying: "Lord! What can I do? . . . people will not obey me. I have been pulling down houses, but the fire overtakes us faster than we can do it!"

By the afternoon the confusion was great. The streets were full of the stink and noise of horses and carts, and people carrying away their possessions. Pepys himself travelled with King Charles and the Duke of

During the Fire in 1666, St. Paul's roof beginning to burn

York by barge to Queenhithe, and was astounded by the "river full of lighters, and boats taking in goods, and good goods swimming in the water." One small boat was weighed down with two virginals.

The *London Gazette* observed that "Many attempts were made to prevent the spreading of it by pulling down houses, and making great intervals, but all in vain, the fire seizing upon the timber and rubbish and so continuing itself, even through those spaces and raging in a bright flame all Monday and Tuesday."

The fire, said to be the greatest since the destruction of Jerusalem, provoked many extreme views. Apart from excited preachers who claimed it heralded the Second Coming of Christ, there were many who thought the fire had been deliberately started. Pepys wrote to Lord Conway: "Without doubt there was nothing of plot or design in all this, though the people would fain think otherwise. Some lay it upon the French and Dutch, and are ready to knock them all on the head wheresoever they meet them; others upon the fanatics . . . others upon the Papists." He said that all the stories of casting fire-balls were found to be mere fictions when they were investigated. He pointed to the fact that no one had made an attempt upon the King or Duke's person, "which might easily have been executed had this been any effect of treason." Dutch and French tourists or residents had to bolt their doors fast, and as Clarendon wrote, "after all the ill usage that can consist in words, and some blows and kicks, they were thrown into prison."

Newgate Prison burning

Sometimes, the mob took the law into their own hands. A contemporary, one Taswell, described how a blacksmith, meeting an innocent Frenchman walking along the street, felled him instantly to the ground with an iron bar, until the blood flowed "in a plentiful stream down to his ankles." Elsewhere, he saw the incensed populace divesting a French painter of all the goods he had in his shop. When they had carried off all his furniture, they pulled his house to the ground, suggesting that he might want to set fire to it as he had everything else.

As the darkness fell on Sunday evening, Samuel Pepys watched the arch of fire in the sky, now a mile long, which showered molten fire drops like golden rain. Back home, he found his own property now in danger, and prepared to flee, "and got my bags of gold into my office ready to carry away, and my chief papers of account also there, and my tallys into a box by themselves." The high wind fanned the flames into a roaring furnace.

A great panic seized the people. Two great disasters, one after the other, seemed too much for the human spirit to bear. It seemed as if the end of the world was at hand. The Earl of Clarendon described how the faces of all the people showed "a wonderful dejection and discomposure," not knowing where they would find one hour's sleep, or safety from the fire. Many people hurriedly deserted their homes and carried away their goods, only to find later that it had not been necessary. Nearly all the refugees made their way to Moorfields, which lay just outside the city; most of them slept on the ground, and put up primitive tents. The King sent several tons of bread and cheese out from the Navy Stores, and the Justices of the Peace were asked to provide whatever food they could. Temporary chapels were built. A reference to Moorfields is made by the poet John Dryden, writing soon afterwards:

> The most in fields like herded beast lie down
> To dews obnoxious on the grassy floor,
> And while their babes in sleep their sorrows drown,
> Sad parents watch the remnant of their store.

Those who fled once more into the countryside received a better welcome than during the year of the plague; hundreds of carts and coaches were sent in to bring people away, and soon the small villages and hamlets around London were packed with refugees. Lord Clarendon was one of many to point out, too late, the need for brick buildings, when it was seen how well brick resisted the fire.

Early on Tuesday morning, Samuel Pepys returned to his house to rescue the last of his belongings. His neighbour, Sir William Batten, "not knowing how to remove his wine, did dig a pit in the garden and laid it there." Pepys followed his example, and buried a large Parmesan cheese as well. That day the fire raged at its height. Evelyn wrote that the stones of St. Paul's Cathedral flew about like grenades, and the molten lead ran down the streets in a stream, and the very pavements were glowing with "fiery redness," so that no horse or man was able to set foot on them. "Nothing but the Almighty power of God" would save the city, "for vaine was the help of man."

In the conflagration many historic buildings had been burned to the ground. The Duke of York, in charge of the fire-fighting, feared for the Tower of London, where a large magazine of gunpowder was stored. With his brother the King he had the surrounding houses pulled down to make an open space across which the flames could not reach. King Charles feared, too, for Whitehall Palace and Westminster Abbey. The Strand, where many of the rich had their houses, was saved, because the wind fell on Tuesday afternoon. But farther east, St. Paul's Cathedral and the Guildhall perished. Vincent described how the lead of the Cathedral roof ran down, as if it had been snow before the sun. The great beams and stonemasonry stones fell with a great noise on to the streets, and crashed down upon Faith Church underneath. Great flakes of stone peeled off from the side of the walls.

On Wednesday, the third day, the worst was over; the entire city had been gutted. To his great relief, Samuel Pepys' own home had been saved. He decided to go out and look at the scene of destruction. Walking into Moorfields, his feet burned on the pavements. Arriving at the massive refugee camp, he watched the homeless in wonderment. "Drank there, and paid twopence for a plain penny loaf; thence homeward, having passed through Cheapside and Newgate Market, all burned, and seen Anthony Joyce's house in fire."

With the exception of old stone churches and similar buildings, the fire destroyed everything in its path, and dozens of people lost their lives trying to escape. It was said that 13,200 houses were destroyed, and 200,000 people turned out into the streets (which shows, incidentally, how crowded seventeenth-century houses in London were).

The King was warmly praised by everyone for his part in fighting the fire. The *London Gazette* described how the King and Duke of York had been seen "frequently exposing their persons with very small attendants, in all parts of the town, sometimes even to be intermixed with those who laboured in the business." Henry Griffith in a letter to Lord Conway agreed. The royal brothers had ridden up and down, giving orders for blowing up houses with gunpowder, to make void spaces for the fire to die in, and standing still to see those orders executed, exposing their persons not only to the crowds but to the "flames themselves, and the ruins of the buildings ready to fall upon them, and sometimes labouring with their own hands to give example to others; for which the people now do pay them, as they ought to do, all possible reverence and admiration."

Rebuilding London

After the fire, the City began to grow rapidly outside the walls; it was found impossible to hold back its expansion any longer. The craftsmen, driven out of their old quarters in the City by growing trade, settled down in the new suburbs. The City of London merged with the City of Westminster. King Charles II ordered that in future no wooden houses were to be built. All new buildings, as far as possible, were to have arched stone cellars. The main streets were to be built wider, and narrow lanes were to be pulled down and rebuilt. Businesses involving the use of fire (such as bakeries) were restricted to certain areas. A

Sir Christopher Wren, architect of the new St. Paul's Cathedral

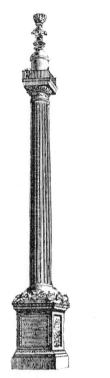

The Monument to London's Fire

survey of the damaged area was to be made. Sir Christopher Wren (1632–1723) was among those who put up schemes for rebuilding the city, but his plan was rejected as most people refused to surrender the right to build on their own foundations.

Men of the time expressed amazement at the new buildings being put up; some even thanked posterity for the fire. Dr. John Woodward of Gresham College told Christopher Wren that however disastrous the Fire of London might have been to the inhabitants, it had multiplied the riches and opulence of the buildings. New common sewers made for sweetness, cleanness, and salubrity, so that London became not only the finest and pleasantest, but the most healthy city in the world. Never again would the city fall victim to the plague.

Thomas Delaune noted in his book *The Present State of London* (1681) that the fire had purged the City; the buildings were infinitely more beautiful, more commodious, more solid than before. London streets were larger and straighter, paved on each side with smooth free stone, and guarded with posts for the benefit of foot passengers. Once, the inhabitants had dwelled in low dark wooden houses, but now they lived in "lofty, lightsome, uniform, and very stately brick buildings." The projecting upper storeys had gone; wooden houses and thatched roofs were no longer permitted. The fire had cleansed the infected soil, the pest-houses and disease-ridden graveyards, and destroyed the polluted water wells most of which were not reopened. In many ways, the picturesqueness of London had been lost; gables, overhanging storeys, and casement windows gave way to a straight façade, and flat square windows with sashes. London had stepped from the seventeenth to the eighteenth century.

Rebuilding St. Paul's Cathedral

7 The Age of Marlborough

THE LIFETIME of John Churchill, first Duke of Marlborough (1650–1722), saw great changes in English life. After the long disruptions of the Civil Wars and the terrors of 1665–66, people wanted above all to live in peace with their families, and devote themselves to their work and leisure, free from the unwelcome interference of Parliament, monarchy, and religious partisans alike. One of the great lessons learned from the experiences of the Civil Wars had been the value of tolerance, which was to become the dominant climate of English life in succeeding generations.

If the monarchy had been restored in 1660, it had been on conditions: the King was at all times to seek the co-operation and goodwill of Parliament, and the Protestant religion was to be defended. Charles II had shown himself to be an agile monarch, and whatever his private sympathies may have been for the Catholic cause, and whatever his inclination towards the doctrine of the divine right of kings, he accepted the need for compromise. But his brother, who succeeded him as James II on 16th February, 1685, was made of a different stuff. Anointed by God, he denied that Parliament had any inalienable rights; and his conscience would never allow him to disavow the Catholic faith, let alone abandon it for ever.

But the Civil Wars had not been fought in vain, and James was soon to find himself in difficulties. In the very first year of his reign an open Protestant rebellion was staged by the Scottish Duke of Argyll and James, Duke of Monmouth, the illegitimate son of Charles II. Monmouth was a very popular man whom many Protestants would have liked to see on the throne. But on 5th July, 1685, Monmouth's small army of 4,000 infantry and 500 horsemen was cut to pieces at the Battle of Sedgemoor by a royal army whose deputy commander was John Churchill. Monmouth himself was quickly executed for high treason, and Judge George Jeffries conducted his notorious tour of reprisal through the West Country – the Bloody Assizes – at which scores of suspected Monmouth supporters were executed.

After the Monmouth rebellion, James II hardened his policies even more, and when his Dutch son-in-law, Prince William of Orange, offered his services to the Protestant English nobility, James's fate was almost sealed. John Churchill himself joined the plot, and commanded

Above James, Duke of Monmouth and *top* the Duke of Marlborough

The Duke of Monmouth *left*, illegitimate son of Charles II was executed *right* for his rebellion against King James in 1685

a rebel army in England, but James had no stomach for battle. Believing that resistance was futile, he despairingly threw the Great Seal into the River Thames and fled to France, effectively abdicating his kingdom in favour of Prince William, who was now to rule jointly with his wife Mary (James's eldest daughter). Twice in a generation the English monarchy had sought to rule in defiance of the people's wishes, and twice the King had been removed. Never again was an English monarch to seek to put on the cloak of absolutism.

After the "Glorious Revolution" of 1688 was over, life returned more or less to normal, and although there were occasional scares and whispers of Popish plots a new and tolerant climate of life was assured. It had been a struggle in which the boldness of Churchill (or Marlborough as he soon became) had played no small part. From this time, new terms begin to be used in political matters – Tory and Whig. It is not our purpose here to study the complex meanings of these terms, except to note that they mirror the growing importance of party politics in English government, and the ascendancy of Parliament in the life of the nation.

The English Countryside

Taking the waters in Bath

England in the age of Marlborough, as we may call the years from 1685, was a pleasant and industrious kingdom, which attracted the praises of many visitors from overseas. The countryside was green, and despite growing deforestation, far more wooded than it is today. The rural population lived for the most part in small scattered hamlets and villages, working as labourers or smallholders on the great estates of the nobility.

One of the most vivid pictures of the English countryside at this time is to be found in the pages of Celia Fiennes's *Journeys* (1702), a classic of English travel literature. Born in 1662 in a family of aristocratic nonconformists near Salisbury, Celia Fiennes was an indefatigable horseback traveller, and devoted her life to chronicling the beauty,

Left The coronation of William and Mary of Orange as king and queen of England in 1689. *Right* The Bill of Rights for the people of England is read to them

wealth, and industry of different parts of the country. In the preface to her book Celia declared that if every lady and gentleman were to set aside some time to exploring their own country, it would greatly promote an understanding of the needs of government, as well as reduce general ignorance, and that home-loving laziness for which the English were notorious.

Celia Fiennes suffered from painful attacks of rheumatism throughout her life, and as a result she visited most of the famous mineral springs of England. She was especially fond of Harrogate in Yorkshire, Knaresborough, and of course Bath, the finest watering-place of all. Here, she records, male and female guides attended the visitors, under the command of a sergeant whom one always had to tip excessively. Iron rings were fixed to the walls of the bath, so that the bathers could steady themselves while standing in the hot stream. The lame and chronically sick would use the hot pump, where the scalding water made it advisable to hire special hat-masks as a protection for the face. This painful cure cost twopence for every hundred pumps.

"Enjoying" the water at Bath

Ladies wore special clothes "made of a fine yellow canvas, which is stiff and made with great sleeves like a parson's gown." When the water swelled up inside the gown it was almost impossible to identify the wearer, especially if they were also wearing one of the hat-masks. Knaresborough did not need such refinements, for the waters were "exceeding cold." But Celia claimed that they healed her chronic headache, and also cured the common cold by sealing up the pores of the skin.

While riding on horseback between the spas, she was very attentive to local industries and standards of life. The cathedral city of Exeter delighted her for the hard work of its people. For twenty miles around, she wrote, people were busy at spinning, weaving, dressing, scouring, fulling, and drying the serges, and all in all conducted over ten thousand pounds' worth of business each week in the city market. She approved, too, of Newcastle upon Tyne, whose clean streets, and well-dressed citizens suggested a "London in miniature." She liked the

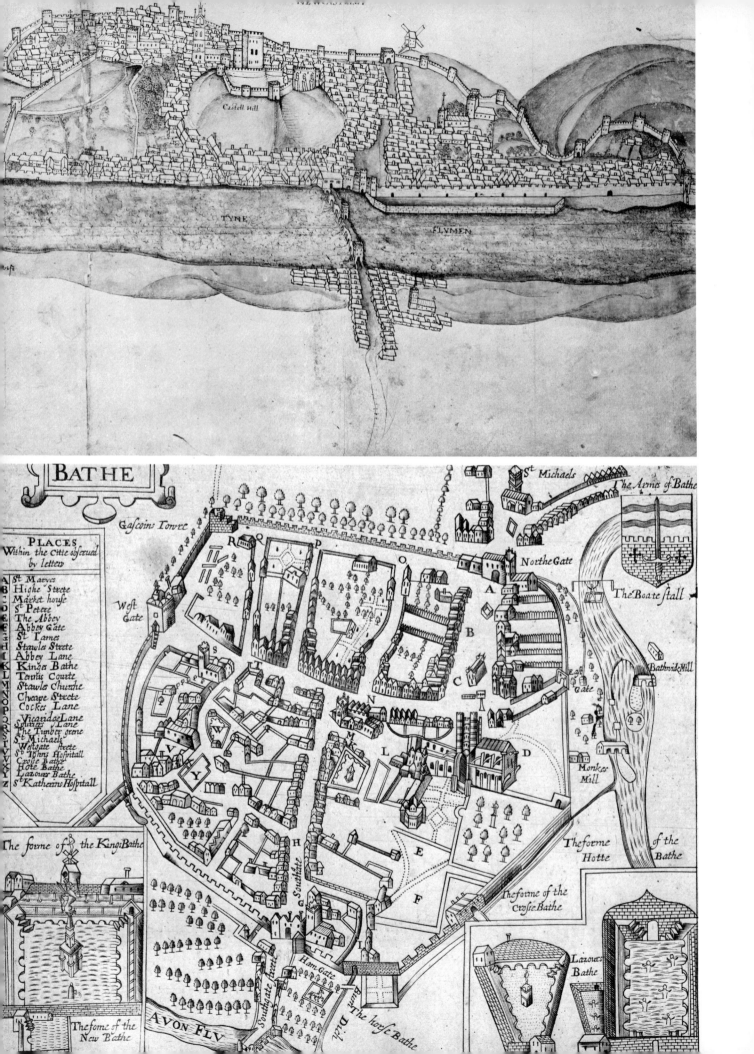

stockings, gloves, waistcoats, and petticoats made at Gloucester ("a low moist place by the Severn"), and also at Nottingham, famous for its lace; and the weaving of flowered silks at Canterbury, the fabrics of which she felt were as beautiful as the cathedral.

As a dissenter with a strong belief in the value of good works she praised the city of Coventry, which spent £3,000 each year for public schools, charity, and "the maintenance of the several public expenses." Few other cities could have boasted the same at this time. The border people of Scotland met with her disapprobation: "They seem to be very poor people, which I imparte to their sloth." She remembered seeing "two or three great wenches as tall and bigg as any woman, who sat hovering between their beds and the chimney corner all idle, doing nothing, or at least was not settled to any work, tho' it was nine of the clock when I came thither, having gone seven long miles that morning."

Her *Journeys* are full of instances of the hazards of road travel in late seventeenth-century England. She found the roads in the Midlands especially bad, once taking eleven hours to ride twenty-five miles. "A footman here could have gone much faster than I could ride, for it was full of sloughs and wet clay." Many times she was thrown headlong by

Heavy coaches with several horses were essential to withstand the bad roads

her horse as they picked their way along slippery unmade chalk or clay tracks. And in the West Country she was attacked by thieves who rushed out from a thicket: a common experience for anyone passing along a lonely track miles from the nearest hamlet.

Throughout the century, little improvement had been made in the road system. Growing complaints were made by the expanding class of private and commercial road users, and in Marlborough's time some new progress was made. The main difficulty had been that the responsibility for upkeep of roads had traditionally rested with the parishes which were far too small a unit for the purpose. Each parish was supposed to maintain its own roads by way of local taxes, but in many cases the local people felt little incentive to help. Rough tracks were often felt quite sufficient for local agricultural and pedestrian purposes. But Parliament now began to introduce a series of measures allowing tolls to be levied on passing traffic, partly to meet this local objection,

A hackney coachman, 1680

and partly to ensure that road improvements were carried out where the traffic was heaviest.

In 1675 John Ogilby published his *Britannia*, the first proper road survey ever carried out in England, commissioned by Charles II. It was a welcome sign that the authorities were beginning to respond to the whole problem of bad communications, which incidentally hampered military security as well.

In Marlborough's time the most familiar sight on the roads was still the cumbersome carrier waggon of former times, but the stage-coach was rapidly making an appearance, too. Indeed, the improvements to both roads and vehicles which followed the publication of Ogilby's survey laid the foundations of that great and prosperous road system of the eighteenth century. The average stage-coach fare at this time was a shilling for every five miles; the stage-coach could cover up to fifty miles a day. The fifty-mile journey from London to Oxford, for example, took twelve hours.

Those who passed through England by road would have found visible signs of progress in agriculture, too, which occupied perhaps nine-tenths of the population. The enterprise of individual landlords had been helped by the steady decline of the old system of common

Left Making hay and *right* a shepherd, pictures from a seventeenth-century book

field farming, and the rise of the more efficient enclosed field. Although the enclosure movement attracted a good deal of opposition by those adversely affected, for example men forced to work as agricultural labourers instead of independent smallholders, it did permit a more economic use of land resources. Enclosure allowed new techniques to be applied on a larger and more productive scale by those who could afford the capital costs involved. Improvements were helped, too, by the growth of population (raising the price of bread), and the influx of cash from the New World, which helped base farming – like town industries – on a capitalist system.

Major innovations included the introduction of clover, and the promotion of turnip cultivation, ideas both imported from Holland in the middle of the century. The techniques of liming and marling the soil, dormant since the fourteenth century, were revived. Records of the time show that patents were steadily being taken out on a whole new range of farming equipment: draining machines in 1628, ploughs in 1623–27 and 1634, and mechanical sowing machines between 1634 and 1639. In the later part of the century these and other machines were coming to be quite widely used, and were the basis of the agricultural revolution led by men like Thomas Coke of Holkham, Jethro Tull, and Robert Bakewell in the eighteenth century. It is noteworthy that few such improvements were recorded in the 1640s and 1650s, the years of the Civil Wars, and years of general agricultural depression.

After the restoration of Charles II in 1660, the newly founded Royal Society played a leading part in encouraging progress. The economic journalist, John Houghton, wrote in his *Collections on Husbandry and Trade* (1690) that "the whole land hath been fermented and stirred up by the profitable hints it hath received from the Royal Society, by which means parks have been disparked, commons enclosed, woods turned into arable, and pasture lands improved . . . so that the food of the cattle is increased as fast, if not faster, than the consumption; and by these means the rent of the kingdom is far greater than ever it was." The lean harvests, which were a feature of the later seventeenth century, played an important part in forcing up prices. Indeed, the rise in food and land prices was one of the most marked features of seventeenth-century life. One bad harvest tended to follow another, as the precious seed corn itself was eaten. Farm rentals soared, as did the freehold value of land; freeholds seemed to have gained most in value being calculated at nearer twenty years' purchase than at fifteen years' as in the reign of James I.

Marlborough's Army

At the Restoration, the New Model Army created by the rebels during the Civil Wars had been progressively disbanded, or nearly so, at the will of Parliament. To ease the task, discharged soldiers had been allowed to enter trades without first serving apprenticeships. But in January, 1661, an insurrection of fanatics, known as the Fifth Monarchy

Scenes of the battle of Blenheim in 1704 when Marlborough defeated the French

Marlborough did much to improve the English army, directing and
encouraging the troops throughout battles

Men, had illustrated the need to keep a small permanent standing
army for the defence of the throne. This force included the Royal
Household regiments known to every Englishman as the Life Guards,
Coldstream Guards, and Royal Scots Guards. In addition, the local
county militia had been reorganized after 1661, maintained by local
grandees according to their property, and commanded by the lord-
lieutenant of each county. As the King was Commander-in-Chief of
both militia and army, he wielded military power comparable to that
of Cromwell himself during the Interregnum.

The life of serving soldiers during the late seventeenth century was
far different from that of later periods. In the first place, Parliament
refused to sanction a code of military law: a soldier who was drunk and
disorderly, or who struck a superior officer, was in theory only liable
to the local magistrates, like any civil offender. In practice, however,
regiments seem to have quietly managed their own discipline; but this
state of affairs, if approved by ordinary soldiers, was a constant menace
to national security. In the second place, both officers and men received
their wages at highly erratic intervals. Charles II had farmed out the
administration of army pay to private contractors at a five per cent
commission, and the abuses and delays involved in the accounting
became a byword of army administration. Until 1663 even private
soldiers had to purchase their employment from the officers. Every
officer throughout most of this period had to pay a substantial sum for
his commission, not only to his regimental colonel, but to the Secretary
at War, one of the Secretaries of State, and also to the new army
hospital at Chelsea, London. Even after all these heavy deductions, an
officer only received a proportion of his pay, and had to wait for a year

or more before receiving his arrears, ambiguously referred to as "gross off-reckonings."

Corrupt, and in many ways inefficient, this was nevertheless the army which Marlborough was to lead to several great victories during the reign of William III: the defeat of the exiled James II at the Battle of the Boyne in Catholic Ireland (1690) and the submission of the French at the Peace of Ryswick (1697). It was the army which, early in the reign of Queen Anne, was to defeat Louis XIV at the Battle of Blenheim (1704), the crowning day in the career of Marlborough, now universally acknowledged as England's greatest military genius. It was the army which in the eighteenth century was to help establish the British Empire overseas.

A Stable Future

It can fairly be said that, for most Englishmen, the seventeenth century closed on an optimistic note. After the turbulent upheavals of the middle years, and the overthrow of James II in the Glorious Revolution of 1688, a more stable balance had been achieved between the monarchy, Parliament, and the people. The wealth of the countryside and of the towns was increasing. With the foundation of the Bank of England (1694) and the New East India Company (1698), commerce was steadily being placed on an expansionist capitalist footing. But perhaps the greatest lesson learned from the long years of religious and social strife was the value of tolerance, the value of that freedom of thought and conscience which Englishmen everywhere have come to prize.

A yeoman of the guard, 1685

Further Reading

MODERN WORKS

Ashley, Maurice, *England in the Seventeenth Century*
Campbell, Mildred, *The English Yeoman*
Clark, Sir George, *The Later Stuarts*
Crofts, J., *Packhorse, Waggon and Post*
Davies, Godfrey, *The Early Stuarts*
Fortescue, Sir John, *History of the British Army*, Vol. I
Hill, Christopher, *Reformation to Industrial Revolution*
——, *Intellectual Origins of the English Revolution*
Hole, Christina, *English Home Life*
——, *The English Housewife*
Mathew, D., *James the First*
Mitchell, R. J., & Leys, M. D. R., *History of London Life*
Ogg, David, *England in the Reign of Charles II*
Wedgwood, C. V., *The Great Rebellion*, 3 vols.

CONTEMPORARY WORKS

Braithwait, Richard, *The English Gentleman* (1641)
Defoe, Daniel, *A Journal of the Plague Year* (1722)
Earle, John, *Microcosmographie* (1628)
Evelyn, John, *Diary* (first published in 1818)
Fiennes, Celia, *Journeys through England* (1702)
Heydon, John, *Advice to a Daughter* (1658)
Hyde, Edward (1st Earl of Clarendon), *History of the Great Rebellion* (first reliable edition 1888)
Osborn, Francis, *Advice to a Son* (1658)
Peacham, Henry, *The Compleat Gentleman* (1661)
Walton, Isaak, *The Compleat Angler* (1653)

Picture Credits

The Publishers would like to express their grateful thanks to the following for kind permission to reproduce copyright illustrations on the pages mentioned: The Trustees of the British Museum, frontispiece, 7 bottom, 19 bottom right, 48 top, 48 bottom right, 92 bottom, 120 top; The British Travel Association, 26 top; J. R. Freeman & Co., 10 centre, 12 top, 13 top right, 14, 15 right and bottom, 19 bottom left, 20 top, 21 bottom, 24 top, 25 top, 26 bottom, 27 centre, 29 bottom, 55 centre, 68 right, 103, 109 right, 121 and 124; The Trustees of the London Museum, 19 top and 112; The Mansell Collection, 7 top, 8, 9, 15 left, 42 right, 69 left, 77, 80 and 119 top left and right; The Trustees of the National Portrait Gallery, 97 bottom, 108 bottom, 117 top and 118 top left; Radio Times Hulton Picture Library, 44 top; The Trustees of the Victoria and Albert Museum, 102 top right and left; The Trustees of the Wallace Collection, 92 top; and The Weaver-Smith Collection, 20 centre, 23 bottom, 45 bottom, 70 top, 70 bottom, 76, 78, 79, 82, 89 right, 91, 92 centre, 94, 96 top, 102 bottom left, 104 top, 118 bottom, 120 bottom, 122 top, 123 left and right, and 125.

Index